THE YEAR OF
You

OTHER WORKS BY SARAH DEBLOCK

The Year of Sarah: From Heartbroken to Happy and the Long Distance In Between

To all seekers of joy,
with gratitude for the teachers and guides who lit the way.

THE YEAR OF
You

A 12-MONTH GUIDE TO AWAKEN YOUR INNER JOY

SARAH DEBLOCK

Published and distributed by Soul Speak Press
An imprint of Merack Publishing

Copyright ©2025 by Sarah DeBlock

ISBN (spiral bound): 978-1-958472-45-3

ISBN: (paperback): 978-1-958472-44-6

This journal is for personal reflection and growth. Some prompts may bring up strong emotions—please move at your own pace and give yourself permission to pause, skip, or come back later.
While these reflections can offer insight and healing, they are not meant to replace the care of a counselor, therapist, or medical professional. If deeper support feels needed, please reach out to a trusted, qualified professional for guidance and care.

CONTENTS

FOREWORD

There's a difference between reading a book and being guided through a journey. The *Year of You* is a journey . . . one that feels like sitting with a trusted
friend who gently reminds you of what you already know deep down: Joy is not
something we chase. It's something we choose.

I've worked with so many people in the wellness world—yoga teachers,
coaches, seekers—and the theme is always the same. We're taught to hustle,
to strive, to measure ourselves by achievement, and to wait for happiness once
"everything lines up." But here's the truth: Life rarely lines up the way we expect.
Joy is not waiting on the other side of perfection. It's available right now, even in
the mess, even in the middle of the unknown.

That's what makes this book so special. It doesn't give you another to-do
list or impossible standard to live up to. Instead, it offers practices, stories, and
reflections that help you soften into what's already here. Month by month, you're
invited to peel back the layers of stress, comparison, and resistance so you can
reconnect with yourself—the part of you that's steady, whole, and ready for
more joy.

What I love most is how doable it all feels. You don't need hours of free time
or some elaborate ritual. You just need a willingness to show up for yourself,
page by page, moment by moment. That's where transformation happens, in
the little choices that add up to a very different way of being.

So as you move through *The Year of You*, I invite you to treat this less like "homework" and more like a conversation with your highest self. Give yourself permission to slow down, to listen, and to remember: You're not here to fix yourself. You're here to reclaim joy, because joy is your birthright.

This isn't just a book. It's a guide back home to yourself. And I can't think of a better journey to take this year.

Arianne Traverso
Business Coach for Holistic Entrepreneurs
Owner of The Yoga Expo

WELCOME

When you do things from your soul,
you feel a river moving in you, a joy.
-RUMI

I'm looking for the seekers.

The souls who ache for a deeper way to live. The lights who sense there is more to life than living the same day on repeat—and who want to finish the year with a fuller heart and greater understanding of themselves.

I'm looking for those who long to live joyfully.

If you are searching for this, then welcome—this journey toward lasting joy is for you. Once you realize that you are love, your life will expand and joy will no longer feel out of reach.

You can live a happy life. You deserve to live a happy life.

I made a promise to myself in middle school that I would grow up to be a happy adult. At the time, I had no idea how I would get there. But I stayed faithful to that promise, allowing life's lessons to unfold and reveal the path one step at a time.

It wasn't easy. I suffered deeply before I discovered the tools that made lasting happiness possible—and I share that journey in my memoir *The Year of Sarah: From Heartbroken to Happy and the Long Distance in Between*. After publishing my story, many readers told me they wanted to create The Year of [Their Name]—to turn their own obstacles into opportunities and steer their lives in a new direction.

They inspired this guided journal, and in these pages I lay out the steps I learned through yoga and lived experience: how to choose joy. Life will never be free of stress or obstacles. You must decide when you will choose happiness, no matter what.

And if there's one thing I know for sure—**happiness is a choice**.

If you are holding this guidebook in your hands, I believe you are ready to choose. You are ready to set aside the old habits and beliefs that have kept you from joy. You are ready to learn the simple, profound practices that can transform your life this year.

This is not a book of short-term strategies. This is not about pouring a glass of wine after work or soothing your heart with late-night sweets. This is about building lasting happiness. Joy is experienced when you raise your frequency—your inner state, the subtle vibration of how you think, feel, and show up in the world.

If you've ever noticed someone moving through life with grace and ease, they're likely attuned to a higher frequency. On the other hand, if you know someone who's always describing their life as feeling stuck, frustrating, or heavy, they're likely moving through denser energy—a lower frequency.

Imagine two people crossing the same river. One is wading through waist-deep water, struggling against the current with every step. The other is swimming with goggles, gliding effortlessly across the surface. Both are in the same environment—but one is moving in alignment with the flow, while the other is fighting it.

The more you align with your natural joy, the more ease you will find on your path. You shift from effort to ease, from resistance to rhythm.

Joy isn't found by grasping for fleeting highs outside of ourselves. It is our natural state of health. It is already within us—always available, waiting for us to align our energy with our truth. Paradoxically, it first requires discipline: slowing down, tuning in, and creating space to feel the reservoir of pure ecstasy that has been inside you all along.

You are worthy of experiencing this joy.

It is your birthright.

It already exists within you in your limitless nature.

There is no better time to choose joy than now.

This is the Year of You!

HOW TO USE THIS GUIDED JOURNAL

Healing is not linear. As you move through this journey, it will be natural to experience ups and downs. This is you spiraling toward your ideal version of yourself, something you'll gain clarity on through these pages. Today you are operating based on everything you know from past lived experiences, and after a year of increasing your frequency, there will be a new version of you.

Throughout your journey, you must remember this is not about fixing yourself; **there is nothing wrong with you**. This guided journal will support you in adding more habits and perspectives that will let you lead your life with more joy.

Healing is also not a destination. When you complete this year, you can move through the exercises again as there is always another level of frequency that you can experience. Everytime you move through these pages, you will see the suggestions from a new point of view.

You can start at any time—there is no need to wait until January. However, I recommend moving through the book from Month 1 to Month 12, as the order is intentionally designed to lead you from foundational, grounded themes toward increasingly expansive and elevated states of being.

Every month you will be guided through three main elements:

1. **A random act of kindness** which will be presented as Spread Joy! Giving back to another is giving back to yourself and will immediately uplift your mood. This is the universal law of reciprocity—the more you give, the more you receive back. Joy is also contagious and this act will inspire the person you bestow the act upon as well as anyone who witnesses the exchange. If we want to live in a joyful world, we must spread joy!

2. **Practices and Reflections** around a theme that supports you in breaking current patterns that block joy.

   There are four weeks of practices and reflections per month. One way to complete these exercises is to block time on your calendar. You can choose to complete the entire week in a few hours on Sunday or spend fifteen minutes per day on the week's lesson. Design the time commitment in a way that is suitable for you. When a month contains five weeks, repeat one week of your choosing that resonates with you.

   At times you may be invited to write; keep a journal or paper nearby to capture your insights.

3. **Gratitude** will be an overarching theme throughout the book as it is a pivotal transformational emotion to cultivate joy. You will practice this daily by writing down three things you are grateful for every night. Feel free to use a favorite notebook or journal or the gratitude pages that have been included at the end of each chapter to help make this habit extremely easy to grow.

Set your space before you begin, signalling that this is a sacred time for you. Light a candle, sip tea, or breathe deeply. Write by hand if you can, and let your thoughts come unfiltered.

If you do nothing else beyond the gratitude pages and Spread Joy!, you will make a noticeable, positive change in your life. But I do hope you choose to engage further—the possibilities for you are limitless as you walk through week by week.

Joy is possible and it can be learned.

SUGGESTED GROUNDING

Calming our nervous system is always the first place to start. This is what makes us feel safe, nurtured, creative, and open to learning.

If you sit down to work on this guided journal and you are feeling anxious, you may not be able to fully focus or receive the benefits. In this circumstance, consider one of these exercises to ground your nervous system before diving right into the pages.

1. Count your breath: inhale 4 counts and exhale 6 counts for 1–2 minutes

2. Repeat to yourself silently or out loud, "I am alright, right now"

3. Go outside. Place your hands on the earth (or imagine doing so if you cannot go outside) and say, "I release this now." Let Mother Nature absorb what you're ready to let go—she can handle anything!

Taking a short amount of time to create coherency for yourself will help you see compound benefits when you complete the practices.

ACCEPT YOUR CIRCUMSTANCES

Comparison is the thief of joy
-THEODORE ROOSEVELT

Bleary-eyed and confused, I rolled over as the 4:00 a.m. alarm beeped long before I had wanted. "Our flight's been canceled" was the first thing I heard from Ryan while my head was still heavy on my pillow. "How do you even know?" I replied in my fog.

As reality set in, we discovered every backup flight option was either a tight timeline or already full. We were supposed to be heading to a dear friend's wedding—a trip we thought would be the *easiest* one that year. Now it looked like we wouldn't make it at all.

I've been flying since I was eight months old. My grandma still tells the story of one of my first flights—my papa walking off the plane with me in one arm and the stroller in the other, baby me just dangling happily, totally content. So I'm very familiar with an airport but that natural baby innocence has often disappeared when a flight is delayed and I have an attachment to where I am headed.

Yet if anything has taught me how to accept the present moment or suffer, it's travel. Especially flying and this morning was no exception.

We pivoted. We threw on clothes, cancelled the Uber, and decided to drive the six hours instead. What followed was a blur of bumper-to-bumper traffic, canceling rental cars, requesting flight ticket refunds, customer service calls, and trying to work from my phone—all while inching toward our destination.

By the time we arrived, we had just enough time to throw on dress clothes and rush to the rehearsal dinner. The bride-to-be greeted us, radiant and glowing. She led us to our seats—right next to her and the groom . . . we weren't in the wedding . . . how could this be?

That's when we learned the maid of honor was stuck in Germany. One bridesmaid's flight was delayed. And another bridesmaid—our friend from DC—had just been in a car accident and her car totaled. Her and her partner were safe, thank goodness, but shaken.

Suddenly, our day's chaos didn't feel like a burden. It felt like a blessing. Because we *were there*. We got to be present for our friend. And later, we were able to drive our carless friends back home.

The best part? That drive back—helping someone out, chatting, laughing, rehashing wedding moments—was one of our favorite parts of the whole trip.

Life rarely goes according to plan. But sometimes, if we're lucky (or just paying attention), we're shown *why* things needed to unfold differently. Not always. But enough times to help us build trust in the unknown.

Whether you feel stuck, hopeful, heartbroken, curious, or uncertain—this month is about honoring the truth of your current season, and letting your desires emerge from *this exact place*. Not from where you think you *should* be, but from where you *are*.

SPREAD JOY!
Genuinely compliment three strangers on things you notice each week this month—on their smile, style, or energy. Notice what happens inside you when you share joy with others.

START WHERE YOU ARE—
THERE IS NO BETTER PLACE

Start where you are. Use what you have. Do what you can.
-ARTHUR ASHE

The best place to start is exactly where you are. Luckily, it's also the only place we *can* start.

This truth has comforted me in many chapters of life—especially the one that inspired the title of my memoir *The Year of Sarah*. At the time, it didn't feel like the beginning of anything special. In fact, I thought my life had taken a turn for the worse.

I had moved to Houston, away from the love of my life, with a fragile plan to join him in Los Angeles after one year. My yoga teacher sensed my resistance and said gently, "If this is where you're planted, why not make it the Year of Sarah?"

That idea—a single sentence—changed everything. It offered me a sense of ownership. Direction. Possibility.

So many of us wait for a "better" moment to begin living—but this moment, this breath, is the only one guaranteed. Accepting our starting point gives us power. When we stop waiting for our life to be different, we begin to fully live it.

This moment is the start of *The Year of You*.

REFLECTION

What would it mean to fully own where you are right now in your life? How would that feel?

_____

_____

_____

_____

If someone said "I am proud of you" right now, how would you respond? Accept it graciously, deny it, softly dismiss it? Can you be proud of yourself right now simply because you got to this point?

_____

_____

_____

_____

PRACTICE

Write a letter to your younger self—tell them how far they have come and how proud they will be of themselves. What do you want to tell them about this chapter? How much peace would that give them?

Notice a part of your body you tend to criticize instead of appreciating it at this moment, as it is.

How much energy do you expend . . .

- on how your body looks versus how your soul feels?
- on how your body looks versus the function it currently provides you?
- on resisting your physical state instead of doing something joyful instead?
- on your body that could go toward feeling freer and more inspired?

This practice can be powerfully transformational. Avoid rushing through it!

GRATITUDE

Each night this week on the Gratitude Pages at the end of this chapter, write three things that you are grateful for about where you are at now.

GRATITUDE IS A TUNING FORK

*Acknowledging the good that you already have in
your life is the foundation for all abundance.*
-ECKHART TOLLE

Gratitude raises our level of consciousness and therefore our inner state of being. It opens the heart, shifts the mind, and tunes us toward resonance with life rather than resistance. When we notice what's already here, our life becomes enough.

It's a potent catalyst that helps train the brain away from a scarcity mindset and toward a resilience and abundance mindset.

REFLECTION

When you reflect on where you are at this moment, is there something that you had wanted in the past, received, and are now taking for granted? List out what comes to mind.

_____

_____

_____

_____

When you show gratitude to someone or express gratitude for something, how does it feel in your body? Where do you feel it in your body?

_____

_____

_____

_____

PRACTICE

Write a list of 100 things you're grateful for—write quickly without overthinking. Include the tiny details: warm socks, the way light hits the floor, a comforting voice.

Choose three items from your gratitude list and write a paragraph about each one. Explore *why* they matter and what they show you about your life.

RESISTANCE IS SUFFERING, ACCEPTANCE IS FREEDOM

*Acceptance of the unacceptable is the
greatest source of grace in this world.*
—ECKHART TOLLE

When we have resistance, we create pain and it is the cause of all suffering. It feels like moving through life with a parking brake on that drains us of all energy.

Acceptance, the antidote, doesn't just mean liking or agreeing with a situation—it means saying, *This is what is*. Being so absolutely honest with ourselves. When we soften into the present moment, we can begin to meet our circumstances with compassion and stop fighting reality. And letting that parking brake release frees a lot of precious energy. It is time to reclaim that energy and turn it into joy!

REFLECTION
What area of your life are you resisting right now?

_____

_____

_____

What emotions come up when you stop trying to change or avoid this part of your life? How can you allow yourself to feel these emotions with compassion? How would this soften your resistance that is creating pain?

PRACTICE

Write about the detours in your life that have brought unexpected blessings. What has surprised you about these events? What beauty or growth has come from an unplanned path?

Set a peaceful timer for 10–15 minutes for this meditation.

- Lie down in **constructive rest** (on your back, knees bent, feet flat on the ground, arms relaxed). Close your eyes.
- Bring to mind a situation or feeling you've been resisting. Instead of analyzing it, **notice where you feel the resistance in your body**—is it in your jaw, your chest, your belly? Now, allow a black ball of smoke to accumulate in the area where you feel resistance. Let it swirl around in this area and get really dark.
- Create a door for this smoke to escape and see it flying out of the door into space.
- Now imagine a gold beam of light shining in this door and filling this space with love, illuminance, and peaceful clarity. Close the door and breathe into that area filled with gold light.
- Let yourself rest here in the golden, healing light for a few more breaths.
- Feel the shift.
- Feel the spaciousness that opens when you stop resisting and start allowing.
- Let this be your reminder: *You are safe to soften. You are safe to surrender.*

THE POWER OF OWNING YOUR STORY

*Owning our story and loving ourselves through
that process is the bravest thing that we'll ever do.*
—BRENÉ BROWN

True self-acceptance begins when we stop disowning parts of ourselves—the messy chapters, the mistakes, the tender moments of growth. It takes courage to say, "This is my life. These are the moments that shaped me." And that courage becomes the root of authentic confidence. When we own our story fully—not just the highlight reel—we find wholeness and discover that our shadow side is what gives rise to our light. And it is connecting to both our shadow and our light that provides us with a feeling of wholeness that gives rise to joy. This is what you have been working toward this month!

REFLECTION
Rather than waiting for a different past or ideal future, what would shift if you honored everything that's brought you here? How might life feel if you stopped hiding the parts you've been judging and instead welcomed them in?

_____

_____

_____

What would change if you truly believed that where you are is enough? How would that feel? This is the start of mastering the yogic principle of *santosha*, contentment.

_____

_____

_____

PRACTICE

In today's rush, we all think too much—seek too much—want too much—
and forget about the joy of just being.
—ECKHART TOLLE

Every day this week:

- Say out loud 3 times: "This is where I am. And it's enough."
- Whisper 6 times: "This is where I am. And it's enough."
- Write down 9 times: "This is where I am. And it's enough."
- Breathe into that truth, no matter how it feels. Let it settle.
- Pause and let the words become your own.

BONUS

Sit quietly with one hand over your heart. Breathe into the truth that *this is where you are, and it is enough.* Write a single sentence that captures what "enough" means for you at this moment. Keep it somewhere you can return to as a grounding touchstone.

GRATITUDE PAGES

_____   _____

_____   _____

_____   _____

_____   _____

_____   _____

_____   _____

_____   _____

_____   _____

_____   _____

_____   _____

_____   _____

_____   _____

_____   _____

GRATITUDE PAGES

_____ _____

_____ _____

_____ _____

_____ _____

_____ _____

_____ _____

_____ _____

_____ _____

_____ _____

_____ _____

_____ _____

_____ _____

GRATITUDE PAGES

_____

_____

_____

_____

_____

_____

_____

_____

_____

_____

_____

_____

_____

_____

MONTH 2

GET INTO YOUR BODY

The mind can lie. The body never does.
—UNKNOWN

Heat built inside me as my shirt clung lightly to my skin in a Crescent Warrior pose. My teacher cued the transition to Warrior Three, and I hinged at my hips, lifting one leg behind me, torso reaching forward until it hovered parallel to the floor.

My leg trembled in midair as I fixed my gaze on one unmoving point, struggling to hold my balance. Everything felt harder than usual, and I had no idea how much longer until Savasana.

This class was part of a yoga retreat, so afterward, we gathered for community reflection. As we went around the circle, my teacher looked at me and said, "You looked very stable this morning, Sarah. That was a great practice."

Stunned, I replied honestly: "My body felt so heavy. I didn't think it was one of my better days."

She nodded and offered something that stuck with me: "Well, sometimes when we finally get back into our body, it can feel heavy."

That gave me a lot to think about.

Had I not been in my body before? Where had I been? Is that what stability feels like when you're fully embodied?

It rang true. I was the kid with bruises all over her shins from constantly running into things—so lost in thought, I didn't notice what was right in front of me. I'd spent many years living mostly in my head.

As a strong academic, I was trained in analytical thinking. I identified so much with my mind, always striving for the next achievement, that I forgot my body had wisdom too—that there was even more of me to listen to.

Even though I had always been active, I hadn't spent much time truly inhabiting my body—listening to its messages, noticing its sensations, or tending to its needs. Yoga changed that. It invited me back into myself and brought my awareness to every corner of my being.

Now I understand: Coming back into the body can feel dense at first. But that heaviness is a powerful sign of reconnection. It's not a burden; it's a return.

And from that place—where all parts of me are accepted and alive—I've found a new kind of stability. A groundedness that lets me stand taller, feel deeper, and experience the present moment more fully.

This month is my invitation to you to return to your body and experience wholeness through your mind, body, and breath.

SPREAD JOY!

Bring in your neighbor's trash cans or rake their leaves without saying a word. Move kindness through your body into the world.

GETTING INTO OUR BODIES

Your body is not a problem to be solved. It is a home to come back to.
—GENEEN ROTH

Your body holds your entire life story: You can start to heal when you listen to your body.

Our bodies are a mirror of our past—our experiences, habits, lifestyle, emotions. When we ignore our body, we are often resisting our past, and when we tune into our body and move from this inner space, we can heal our past and transform the present moment for a more joyful future. Why? Because we are no longer going to live the same day over and over again.

PRACTICE
BODY SCAN MEDITATION
Spend five minutes slowly moving your awareness through your body from head to toe. Don't try to change anything—just notice. What do you sense—heat, cold, tingling, heaviness, space, tension?

End with the mantra:

I witness sensations and embrace the fullness of being alive.

REFLECTION

When you listen to your body without judgment, what do you notice? Where are you holding tension? Where do you feel most at ease?

_____

_____

_____

_____

Are there any sensations that often repeat? Might these be messages from your body trying to tell you something?

_____

_____

_____

_____

Transformational Ritual: Write a short letter of appreciation to your body for all the ways that it supports you.

_____

_____

_____

_____

LISTENING TO WHAT THE BODY IS SAYING

To be grounded is to be in touch with the earth and in touch with your body.
And the more connected you are to your body, the more alive you feel.

—TARA BRACH

Our body speaks to us constantly. Symptoms, discomfort, and even ailments are the body's way of communicating. This week, we'll explore how to listen more attentively and understand what the body is trying to tell us. When we tune into these signals, we empower ourselves to take meaningful action for healing and well-being.

If you can embody these messages, instead of feeling like you are fighting your body, you will become friends and a life-long partner with your body. Pain and symptoms are a gift that show you what is truly needed for healing.

PRACTICE
LISTENING TO THE BODY'S MESSAGES
Sit comfortably and gently close your eyes. Scan your body from head to toe for at least 5 minutes. Pay attention to any areas of tension, discomfort, or ease. Take note of these sensations without judgment, and simply observe. Now move onto the next practice.

5 QUALITIES OF PAIN MEDITATION

This meditation focuses on the 5 Qualities of Pain, designed to help you observe pain or sensations with mindfulness in order to cultivate greater mental resilience and healing. You can repeat the meditation more than once focusing on the same area or a different one each time. The instructions are written below, or listen to a guided recording at bit.ly/5QualitiesPain.

- Find a place where you can sit comfortably, high on your sit bones. This can be a meditation pillow on the floor or on the edge of a chair.
- Place the backs of your hands on your thighs with palms facing upward. Notice if you need to make any final adjustments to your sustainable seat.
- Closing your eyes, draw awareness to your breathing.
- Become aware of the quality of your breath. Allow your breath to become full and deep—lengthening and deepening your inhale and exhale.
- Starting at the top of your head, begin to scan your body, becoming aware of areas of pain, tension, or sensation.
- Allowing your awareness to settle in on one of the areas you noticed, assign that area of pain, tension, or sensation a quality of movement. Maybe it feels heavy like a rock or like it's jumping around like a frog.
- Assign this area a temperature—cold, cool, warm, hot.
- Assign it a color, any color—the first one that comes to mind.
- Assign this area a shape—any shape at all.
- Now, in your mind's eye, see this pain, tension, sensation with its qualities of movement, temperature, color, and shape sitting in the palm of your outstretched hand.
- Give it space.
- Allowing it to be.
- Allowing it to be.
- Shift your awareness back to your breathing—silently saying to yourself, *Breathing in, breathing out.*
- When you are ready, bring your palms together at the heart center and take a cleansing breath. Mindfully open your eyes.

REFLECTION

Choose any physical symptoms or health issues you've been experiencing and ask yourself:

- When do I notice them the most? Certain times of the day? Certain activities? When certain emotions are present?
- How do these symptoms feel emotionally—are they linked to stress, anxiety, or any other feelings?
- What do I believe these symptoms might be trying to communicate to me about my mental, emotional, or physical state?

_____

_____

_____

_____

_____

Identify one specific symptom or discomfort that you've noticed and explore what your body might be trying to communicate through it. What action do you need to take to listen to this message?

_____

_____

_____

_____

SHAKE IT OUT

Motion is emotion. You can use your body to change your mind.
—TONY ROBBINS

Movement is medicine. Emotions are energy in motion, and they are only an issue when they stop moving. This is when they get lodged in the body, and we may experience symptoms like tight shoulders, heartburn, or headaches. When we move, we allow emotions to flow once again. This fluidity of movement enables us to be able to consciously choose joy.

PRACTICE
DANCE AND PLAY
Have a 10-minute solo dance party. Choose music that makes your body want to move and puts a smile on your face. Let your body lead. No choreography, no mirror—just joy.

Hot Tip: Give yourself the gift of a dance party regularly!

Continue to move through the week—sing in the car, wiggle your shoulders while brushing your teeth, be silly, and watch how joy enters into your daily life!

REFLECTION

How do you feel after moving like this? Where do you feel more open or free?

_____

_____

_____

_____

What emotions arose when you let yourself move freely? Did you notice any areas that were harder to move?

_____

_____

_____

_____

Were you able to feel a shift in energy after a short dance party?

_____

_____

_____

_____

MOVE WHAT MATTERS

The movement you need is the one you're not doing.
—GABRIELLE ROTH

We can consciously shift our emotional and energetic state through posture and breath. Every physical movement has an energetic blueprint that shapes our consciousness—this is the basis of yoga asana (postures). It's also why the phrase "fake it until you make it" holds truth.

When you're seeking more confidence, channel JLo—head high, heart open, no apologies. When you're seeking more joy, be the child at the custard shack—laughing, stunned by the abundance of choices, skipping down the street.

Our body, mind, and spirit are not separate—they are in constant conversation. When we move with intention, we don't just change how we feel in the moment—we begin to reshape who we are becoming.

TRY THESE JOYFUL MOVEMENTS:
- Smile—feel your whole face soften
  - If this is difficult from feelings of sadness, place a pencil lightly between your teeth. This will cause the corners of your mouth to turn upward, and you will get the same energetic effect as smiling.
- Stand tall—arms overhead
  - This naturally signals to our brain that we are happy! Think about what you do if your favorite sports team wins or your child makes a soccer goal—arms in the air!

- Laughter
  - Laugh simply because! You don't need a reason.
- Breath of Joy
  - This is a 3-part inhale followed by an exhale with arm movement exercise.
    - ◊ Begin by standing with your feet hip width apart and knees soft.
    - ◊ Inhale a third of your capacity as you sweep your arms out in front of you shoulder height, palms up.
    - ◊ Inhale another third of your capacity as you sweep your arms out beside you to shoulder height.
    - ◊ Inhale completely as you sweep your arms overhead.
    - ◊ Exhale fully with a ha sound as you fold forward sweeping your arms behind you.
    - ◊ Complete at least 3 rounds consecutively.

For a video of Breath of Joy, you can see me demonstrating it at this link: bit.ly/breathofjoydemo.

Mantra

I am allowed to feel good in my body.
I feel, I honor, I release.

REFLECTION

What movements consistently bring you into joy or presence? How can you add more of them into your daily life?

_____

_____

_____

Have you been moving enough to experience joy and maintain freedom in your body? Block off time on your schedule for this movement.

_____

_____

_____

BONUS

Find a yoga class that you can attend consistently to ensure you are addressing the body, mind, and breath and allowing emotions to be processed. Seek a teacher that has a teacher themself for continuous learning and who emphasizes the breath in class.

GRATITUDE PAGES

_____

_____

_____

_____

_____

_____

_____

_____

_____

_____

_____

_____

GRATITUDE PAGES

_____
_____
_____
_____
_____
_____
_____
_____
_____
_____
_____
_____
_____

GRATITUDE PAGES

_____   _____

_____   _____

_____   _____

_____   _____

_____   _____

_____   _____

_____   _____

_____   _____

_____   _____

_____   _____

_____   _____

_____   _____

MONTH 3

ALLOW YOUR EMOTIONS

You cannot selectively numb emotion. When we numb the painful emotions,
we also numb the positive emotions.
—BRENÉ BROWN

I straightened my spine clueless to what was coming next.

I shifted around on my leopard-print zafu meditation cushion in front of my altar to find my ideal seat as I do every morning. With my mala gracefully draped over my right hand high enough to not let the beads touch the floor—a quiet ritual I'd practiced for years—I started to feel lighter with each mantra repetition. The familiar tingling sensation that normally stopped at my heart rose further toward the crown of my head . . . and kept rising. My entire chest space felt expanded and suddenly an energetic force was lifting my spine up to where there was no physical exertion to sit upright.

This was the ordinary part.

Then it happened.

Joy.

Not just sunny weather or I found the best matcha-latte joy—I mean soul-jolting, all-worldly-matters-melt-away joy. It moved up my spine from deep within me and encompassed my entire being. A level of euphoria that far surpassed my daily feeling of happiness. I could have stayed in this bliss as long as I wanted, soaking up a new miraculous way to live . . .

. . . but, no, what did I do?

I opened my eyes!

Yes. I let it all go, literally in the blink of an eye. The feeling had startled me and if pure bliss can feel uncomfortable, it somewhat did. Almost like an inner voice whispering to me, *Are you allowed to feel this good?* And, *you need to come back to reality!*

This morning was an eye opener for me literally and spiritually on multiple levels. I had spent years knowing that I needed to feel my feelings, especially anger, grief, or fear, but I had never considered that I may suppress joy—the emotion I most sought!

And yet, being on the other side, it all makes sense. Emotion is simply energy in motion and all emotions can reach a frequency level that we are not accustomed to feeling, and I was not calibrated to this amount of pure joy for merely existing. It felt foreign.

So now I practice to allow all emotions to run through me, so that when joy returns swinging the door open, I can greet her with a smile and wide open arms—giving myself full permission to live in this realm.

This month, we'll be practicing just that: creating space for the *entire* emotional spectrum so that joy doesn't feel like an intruder, but a welcome guest who's finally found her way home.

SPREAD JOY!

Let someone go ahead of you in line at the store or in traffic. Especially when you feel impatience or frustration arise, soften and choose kindness.

FEEL TO HEAL

The only way out is through.
—ROBERT FROST

Emotions are not problems to fix; they are signals to listen to. Emotional freedom begins when we release the habit of labeling feelings as good or bad and instead honor them all as meaningful messengers. The first step toward this freedom is learning to name what we're truly feeling at any given moment.

This week, give yourself permission to feel—fully, honestly, and without judgment.

PRACTICE

There is intentionally only one practice this week so that you have time to implement this every day because it is transformative when truly practiced.

Set a reminder to pause every 4 hours and ask: *What am I feeling right now? Where do I feel it in my body?*

- Name the emotion without judgment. To gain the most from this practice, try to identify a true emotion rather than a state of being. For example, words like *stressed* or *tired* describe states of being versus emotions. In yoga philosophy, there are nine main emotions (rasas): joy, sadness, fear, anger, disgust, love, courage, wonder, and calmness.

- Use the emotion wheel below to help you find the word that best matches what you're feeling. Once you've identified it, gently say out loud: **This emotion is welcome here.**

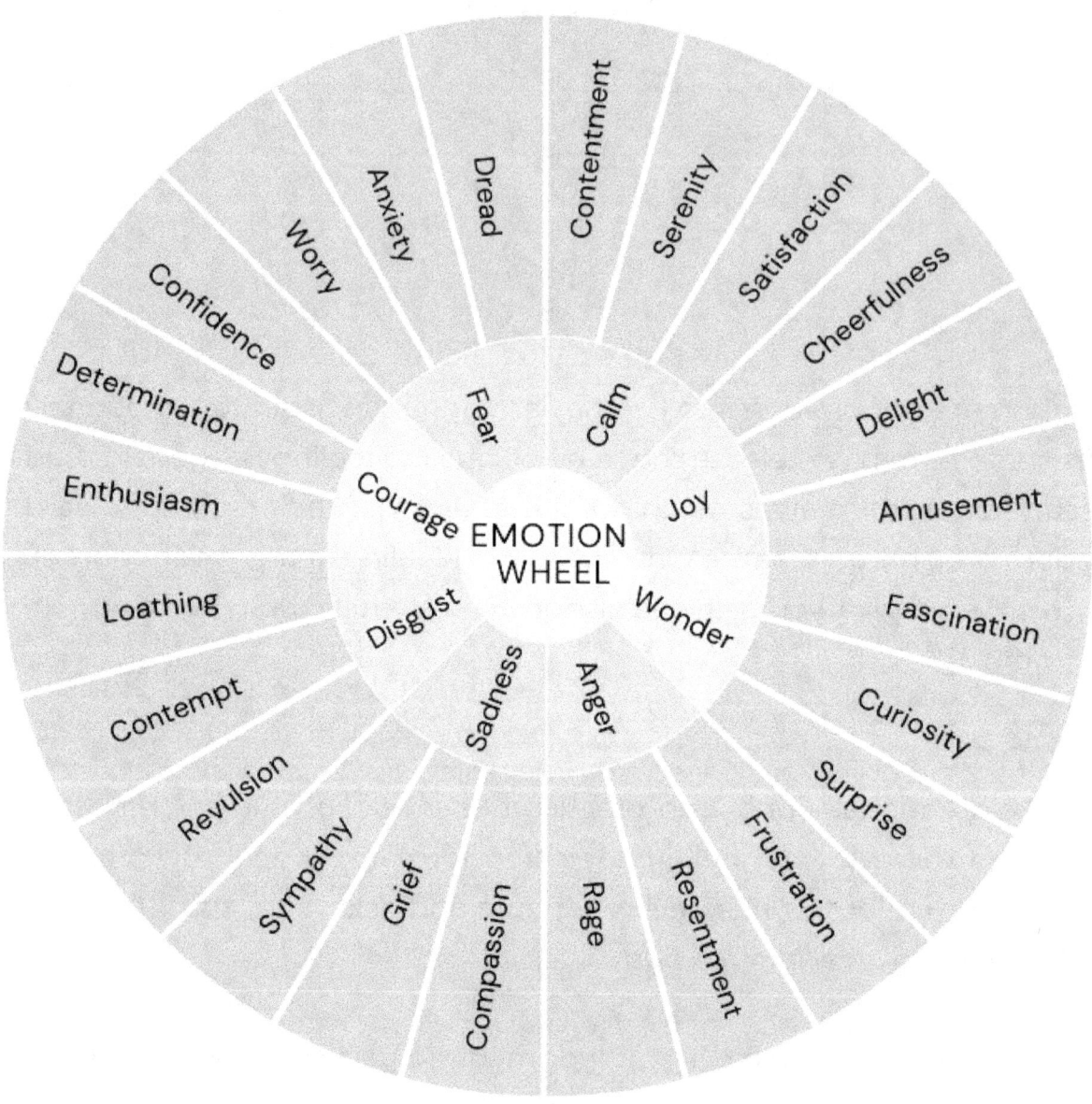

REFLECTION

How difficult was it to name your emotion each time you paused? Did you feel connected or disconnected to how you were feeling?

_____

_____

_____

_____

When was the last time you truly let yourself feel sad, angry, or joyful without trying to change it?

_____

_____

_____

What emotion do you usually try to suppress or ignore? What do you fear might happen if you allow that emotion to surface?

_____

_____

_____

_____

HONORING EMOTIONAL PARADOX

There's no one thing that's true. It's all true.
—ERNEST HEMINGWAY

As we saw in Week 1, knowing what we are feeling is the first step and some-times that can be complex since you can feel sorrow and still laugh. You can grieve and still love. Emotional wholeness doesn't mean feeling one mood at a time—it means making space for the full spectrum, often with more than one emotion at once.

All parts of you—including the messy, the shadowy, the emotional—deserve love. You are allowed to hold conflicting emotions. That's not confusion—it's humanity. One emotion does not cancel out another. This is the beauty and complexity of the human potential to feel.

We cannot wait for the hard parts of life to pass to allow ourselves to feel joy. We are allowed to feel great during hard and messy times as well.

PRACTICE

Tears are released emotion made visible—they reveal how joy and sorrow are deeply intertwined. Let that sink in . . .

Have you ever considered the beauty of how tears are for opposing emo-tions? When was the last time you allowed yourself to cry? Let yourself cry this week—whether it's a tear over a song or a full release.

Notice how you can cry tears of joy or tears of sorrow. Which is needed right now?

At the end of one day this week, write down two seemingly opposing emotions you felt. (Example: "I felt grateful and lonely.") Notice how one does not have to negate the other. Ask yourself: *How can I hold space for both emotions at once without needing to 'choose' between them?*

This is a powerful practice in learning how to hold a space of joy even in the presence of seemingly opposite feelings or circumstances. You are building the muscle of balance- equanimity.

Choose one emotion you've been resisting and write it a letter. Invite it to speak freely.

REFLECTION

What emotion do you judge yourself for feeling? Does this lend you to feel some emotions are more valid than others, or for this emotion to grow stronger or softer?

_____

_____

How does feeling two opposing emotions simultaneously add to your definition of living in wholeness?

_____

_____

Can you recall a time when laughter and tears showed up together? What wisdom was present in that moment?

_____

_____

_____

EMOTIONS ARE VISITORS

This being human is a guest house. Every morning a new arrival . . . Welcome and entertain them all.

—RUMI

Emotions come and go—they are not who you are. All of your emotions are valid—but emotions do not equal truth. They are simply a reflection of our past thoughts and reactions that are passing by as feelings.

Joy is a spiritual practice because it requires us to get quiet and see past all of our emotions to feel its Truth at our inner core.

PRACTICE
Read or recite the poem **"The Guest House" by Rumi**.
This being human is a guest house.
Every morning a new arrival.

A joy, a depression, a meanness,
some momentary awareness comes
as an unexpected visitor.

Welcome and entertain them all!
Even if they're a crowd of sorrows,
who violently sweep your house
empty of its furniture,

still treat each guest honorably.
He may be clearing you out
for some new delight.

The dark thought, the shame, the malice,
meet them at the door laughing,
and invite them in.

Be grateful for whoever comes,
because each has been sent
as a guide from beyond.

—From *The Essential Rumi*, translated by Coleman Barks.
Reprinted by permission.

Visualize emotions as guests arriving at your front door. Practice welcoming each one, then letting them leave. You can reference the emotion wheel again to spark ideas of how many emotions could come to your door.

- When you feel a strong emotion, whisper: *"This too is passing through."*

Is there a certain emotion that you try to slam the door shut on in order not to feel its energy?

- The next time this emotion visits, invite them in to sit and count to 90 as you feel the energy in your body. Remember from Week 1, that you must first feel it before you can heal it. If the emotion still is uncomfortably strong after counting, then you can ask it to walk back out the door.

REFLECTION

What emotion keeps overstaying its welcome at your door, and what might help it move along? Drawing a picture representation? Stream of consciousness journaling? Speaking a truth? A dance party?

_____

_____

_____

_____

How have your emotions taught you about what you value or need?

_____

_____

_____

_____

What would emotional freedom feel like to you?

_____

_____

_____

_____

SUCCESS AND FAILURE ARE THE SAME

I have not failed. I've just found 10,000 ways that won't work.
—THOMAS EDISON

Success and failure are both part of the path—they carry no moral weight. This week we will focus on neutralizing judgement around success and failure to experience how freeing that can be. Without one the other does not exist, and being attached to them can lead to perpetually feeling elated only to crash back down to despair.

When the ability to mentally neutralize results is achieved, you will experience joy more often; you will know that you are creating and experimenting to see what works and what doesn't. You will view it as a game. The people we view as the most successful have failed the most because often they have made the most attempts and kept moving forward.

PRACTICE
At the end of the day, reflect on a high and a low. Write them both down and then write underneath these 9 nine times: *Both were part of my Becoming.*

Practice the mantra **"Neti Neti"** (It is neither this, nor that) when you feel stuck in labeling something as good or bad. Say this mantra as many times as you need throughout each day. This will help reduce the emotional charge around how you perceive an outcome.

Often so much more is happening than we know and the larger picture of an outcome could very much be in our favor. Just because something appears good or bad to you does not mean that is so. *Neti Neti*—it is neither this, nor that!

REFLECTION

Recall a moment you "failed," and identify what wisdom came from it. What positive outcomes would not have occurred had you "succeeded."

_____

_____

_____

_____

Do you remember this lesson better than you would have if you "succeeded"?

_____

_____

_____

_____

Where do you tie your worth to performance?

_____

_____

_____

_____

How would you move through life differently if you saw every outcome as part of the game like an experiment?

_____

_____

_____

_____

BONUS

Close your eyes and imagine yourself as you were at your most tender this month. Offer that version of you a kind phrase, as you would to a dear friend. Write down the words you most needed to hear, and return to them whenever your heart needs softening

GRATITUDE PAGES

GRATITUDE PAGES

_____   _____

_____   _____

_____   _____

_____   _____

_____   _____

_____   _____

_____   _____

_____   _____

_____   _____

_____   _____

_____   _____

GRATITUDE PAGES

_____ _____

_____ _____

_____ _____

_____ _____

_____ _____

_____ _____

_____ _____

_____ _____

_____ _____

_____ _____

_____ _____

_____ _____

CLARIFY YOUR HEART'S DESIRE

Let yourself be silently drawn by the strange pull of
what you really love. It will not lead you astray.
—RUMI

I ended the call with a click of a button, grabbed my book in the middle of the afternoon, and leisurely made my way to the couch. Curling up with both legs tucked to the right, I leaned on the arm rest and let the sun's rays warm my face as they streamed through the window.

"That's a pretty nice work day," my husband Ryan remarked as he walked by. He happened to be working from home that day, a rare occurrence, and I could tell he wanted to make sure I fully appreciated the stellar setup I had.

Work from home. Good salary. Supportive supervisor. Ample leisure time between calls.

It was a dream—no doubt *someone's* dream. Someone who would've snatched my job in a heartbeat, no questions asked. Yet my husband and I both knew it wasn't fulfilling me. I felt limited, dull, unenthused.

Sure, reading in the afternoon was great, but it was only because I couldn't leave my computer. I had to be available in case a question came in—ready to respond instantly to prove I was present. I felt tethered, craving the kind of freedom where I could grab a coffee with a friend or head to the gym midday, knowing I could still be counted on to get my work done afterward.

At a women's leadership conference I attended, an impressively successful business owner once said, "Entrepreneurship is a moment of insanity that lasts a long time." Ryan's comment felt like a gentle nudge, a kindly veiled question: Was I really wanting to head toward insanity?

Sitting there, sun-kissed and calm with all the luxuries I could need, I paused on this statement that I had turned into a question. My mind loudly reminded me that I loved this security. How great it was to feel safe and stress free!

But then I remembered how I felt bored and my heart whispered: *You know there's more. You'll have regrets.*

I was wandering toward insanity, but procrastinating to create my moment.

It was time to choose: comfortable and complacent, or uncomfortable and passionate.

My heart had been whispering for a while now—urging me to go for my dream. To start my own business. To create a vibrant life where I'd wake up excited on Mondays and leave no regrets behind.

I knew what I wanted. That was a critical first step.

But boy, did owning my moment scare me.

This month's focus is of utmost importance: If you don't know what you want, then you can't direct your energy in that direction or experience the joy of it fulfilled. In these weeks, you'll have the opportunity to clarify and be deeply honest with yourself about what you truly desire. Let what's real rise to the surface—before its potential gets clouded by logistics, what-ifs, or the how-tos.

SPREAD JOY!

Offer a small kindness connected to what you love most. If you love flowers, leave a flower for someone. If you love baking, share a baked good.

DISCOVERY—DESIRES AND VALUES

When your values are clear to you, making decisions becomes easier.
—ROY E. DISNEY

Can you recall the feeling of making a decision that felt expansive, light, or simply "right" in your body? That was the power of being aligned with your true desires and values. When choices feel confusing or heavy, it's often because your deeper wants or nonnegotiable values aren't yet clear. This week, you'll explore what matters most to your heart so you can move forward with clarity and shape your life in an intentional, joyful direction.

PRACTICE
MIND MAP YOUR DESIRES
Explore what you most long for in the following areas by mind mapping. For each category, allow thoughts, associated words, and feeling tones to arise and add these in adjacent circles. You may need to close your eyes to feel what you want your life to look like or reflect on some of your happiest memories to identify patterns that bring you joy.

- Work
- Relationships
- Health
- Spirituality
- Recreation
- Wealth

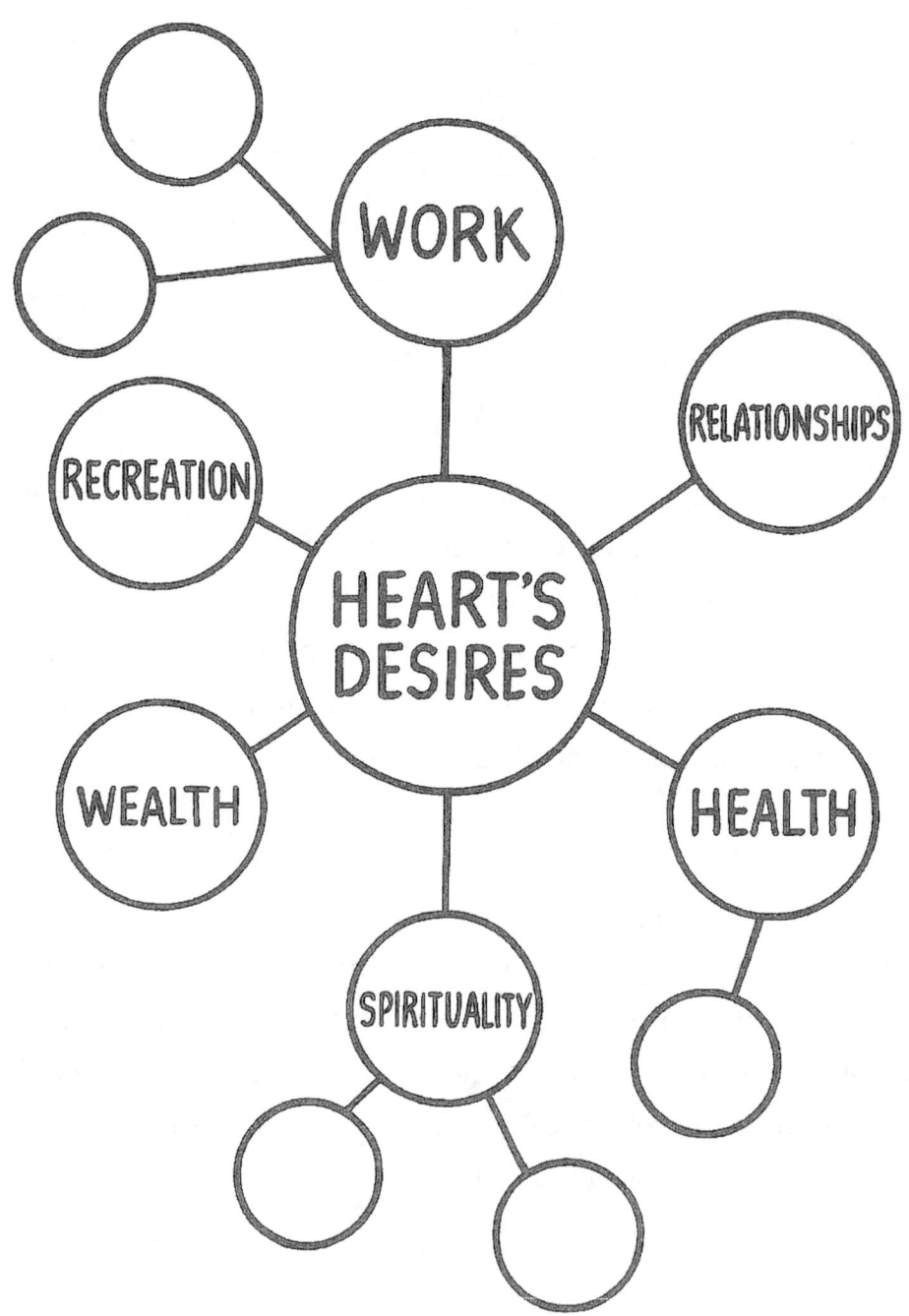

REFLECTION

Did you create these within your current money and time limitations?
What can you add when you let yourself dream bigger beyond your current
paradigm? Create another mind map if you find that there is a lot more to
explore when you drop immediate limitations.

_____

_____

_____

_____

PRACTICE
IDENTIFY YOUR VALUES

Circle all the values that most resonate with you from the list below. Scan over
each without taking too much time to pause and select the ones that immediately stand out.

Integrity	Compassion	Creativity	Freedom	Presence
Kindness	Courage	Growth	Balance	Gratitude
Connection	Honesty	Trust	Joy	Simplicity
Service	Curiosity	Humility	Peace	Vitality
Love	Mindfulness	Wholeness	Patience	Responsibility
Authenticity	Justice	Forgiveness	Resilience	Empathy
Generosity	Flexibility	Confidence	Harmony	Intuition
Community	Respect	Adventure	Clarity	Loyalty

Purpose	Self-care	Acceptance	Boldness	Playfulness
Open-mindedness	Hope	Determination	Cooperation	Groundedness
Inclusion	Faith	Reflection	Wonder	Wisdom
Accountability	Listening	Belonging	Sustainability	Bravery
Reverence	Stillness	Equanimity	Optimism	Devotion
Dignity	Vision	Collaboration	Healing	Centeredness
Transparency	Transformation	Interdependence	Altruism	Adaptability
Kind Speech	Awe	Fairness	Maturity	Stability
Empowerment	Surrender	Service	Curiosity in Spirit	Flow
Initiative	Grace	Trustworthiness	Renewal	Truthfulness

Of the ones you circled, select the five values that feel most essential to you right now:

1. _____

2. _____

3. _____

4. _____

5. _____

REFLECTION
How do these values make you feel?

_____

_____

_____

_____

Do they bring any clarity to areas where you feel unfulfilled?

_____

_____

_____

_____

ALIGNMENT—HEART CLARITY

Don't ask yourself what the world needs. Ask yourself what makes you come alive, and go do that. Because what the world needs is people who have come alive.
—HOWARD THURMAN

When your values and desires work together, you feel a sense of harmony that is like truth in motion. Alignment helps you turn longings into a clear compass for living with joy. Without this clarity, you might achieve goals that look good on the outside yet leave you feeling unfulfilled—like working tirelessly for outer success when what you truly long for is more connection, rest, or creative freedom. This week, you'll explore how to tap into your heart's clarity—through the activities that make you feel alive, the quiet truths revealed by jealousy, and the desires that reflect your deepest values. By noticing these connections, you'll uncover the path that feels most authentic and energizing for you.

REFLECTION
VALUES AND DESIRES ALIGNMENT
Do your current desires align with your selected values?

_____

_____

_____

Does this change how you feel about any of your desires?

_____

_____

_____

A PEEK INTO JEALOUSY (YES, IT'S A CLUE!)
Are you jealous of anyone or anything right now?

_____

_____

_____

What could this be revealing about your true desires? About what you seek?

_____

_____

_____

WHAT MAKES YOU COME ALIVE?
What activities or moments bring you the most joy, energy, or excitement?

_____

_____

_____

Why do you think these make you feel so alive? What can you learn from these about what you want?

_____

_____

_____

PRACTICE

Schedule one of those activities that makes you feel most alive in the next week. Notice how it lights up your soul and contemplate what aspect of this activity connects with you.

What is your heart asking for? Repeat the reflection questions for the "What Makes You Come Alive?" section after having just done the activity—have any answers changed or evolved?

PERSPECTIVE—SOUL TRUTHS

And the day came when the risk to remain tight in a bud was more painful than the risk it took to blossom.

—ANAÏS NIN

In the busyness of daily life, it's easy to drift off course without realizing it. Distractions arise, other people's opinions weigh in, and competing goals can pull your attention in many directions at once. One way I pause and recalibrate is by asking myself: *At the end of my life, what will truly have mattered most?* This simple reflection gives me a higher perspective and helps me recalibrate instantly to see whether my choices are aligned with my heart's deepest desires—and with the joy I wish to cultivate.

REFLECTION

Imagine you are at the end of life with only a single day left. Which of your desires will have been most important to fulfill?

_____

_____

_____

_____

Does the way you are spending your time now align with that fulfillment?

PRACTICE

The word courage comes from the Latin *cor*, meaning heart. For 5 minutes, sit quietly and place your awareness at the space of your heart. Breathe gently in and out, letting each breath soften you. Then ask yourself:

- *What is my heart asking me to be brave about?*
- *Where am I being called to act, even if fear or uncertainty is present?*

EMBODIMENT—VISIONING FORWARD

Create the highest, grandest vision possible for your life,
because you become what you believe.
—OPRAH WINFREY

If you want to create a certain kind of life for yourself, you must begin by drawing the future into the present moment. That's our focus this week: first clarifying the life you long to feel and live, and then practicing how to experience it *now*. This kind of intentional "time travel" plants the seeds of your future joy in today's soil. Over time, you will find yourself standing fully in the joy you envisioned, knowing that it blossomed because you chose to live your future in the present.

REFLECTION
ENVISION YOUR FUTURE SELF
Use the below questions to create a mind map or list of what your life looks like at the end of the year:

What dreams have been realized?

Consider the goals, intentions, or desires you set at the start of the year. Which ones have come to fruition? How does it feel to see them realized, and what impact do they have on your daily life and sense of fulfillment?

_____

_____

_____

_____

Physical health

Imagine your body at its healthiest and strongest. How do you feel physically each day? What habits, exercises, or routines have contributed to your well-being? Have you created a body that feels strong, nourished, and cared for?

_____

_____

_____

_____

Energy levels

Reflect on your overall energy and vitality. Are you waking up feeling refreshed and motivated? How do you sustain focus and enthusiasm throughout your day? What practices or routines have helped you maintain high energy?

_____

_____

Relationships

Visualize the quality of your relationships—family, friends, colleagues, or romantic connections. Are they nurturing, supportive, and aligned with your values? Have you nurtured deeper connections, welcomed new friendships, or experienced greater harmony with loved ones?

Career or creative work

Think about your professional or creative life. How does your work reflect your passions, skills, and purpose? Have you taken bold steps toward your passions, celebrated milestones, or expressed yourself in ways that feel fulfilling?

Note how achieving each of these would feel. Can you fully FEEL it now? Allow yourself to feel this reality *right now*! Sit with this feeling.

PRACTICE

Write a Letter to Your Future Self

Write in present tense as if it's the end of the year and your dreams have been realized.

Describe:

- Where you are
- What you've experienced
- How you feel

Reread this letter every day for 30 days: This is a vital step toward building a joyful life, and the longer you stay with it, the more its benefits will compound!

BONUS

Sit in stillness and ask your heart, *What do you long for most right now?* Let the answer rise gently, without forcing. Write one sentence that begins, *My heart is calling me toward . . .* and honor whatever comes through.

GRATITUDE PAGES

_____

_____

_____

_____

_____

_____

_____

_____

_____

_____

_____

GRATITUDE PAGES

_____   _____

_____   _____

_____   _____

_____   _____

_____   _____

_____   _____

_____   _____

_____   _____

_____   _____

_____   _____

_____   _____

_____   _____

GRATITUDE PAGES

_____   _____

_____   _____

_____   _____

_____   _____

_____   _____

_____   _____

_____   _____

_____   _____

_____   _____

_____   _____

_____   _____

_____   _____

EXPAND YOUR PERSPECTIVE

"The difference between a mountain and a molehill is your perspective."
—AL NEUHARTH

I grew up with a mom with an expansive perspective. The word *no* did not exist in her vocabulary. For her, the impossible was a challenge to be tackled.

I was continually reminded that I could do anything. Yes, anything is possible.

She'd even constantly tell me that I didn't know what I wanted to do for a living because it didn't yet exist. *I would have to create it.* Yikes! That sounded big and scary to me as a kid. But it turns out she was right, as I am now an entrepreneur.

So when I said I wanted to model in high school, she supported me. Well actually, I had wanted to model for years but she feared exposing me to the toxic body image culture, and when I turned seventeen, she finally agreed. That's when she supported me full force. Another thing to know about my mom—she believes if you are going to do something, then you should put forth your full effort.

The next thing I know we are on vacation in San Diego and she is pointing to a flyer at a coffee shop. A boutique fashion designer was searching for runway models for their spring season collection. "You have to do this, Sarah! It will be great for a modeling resume in New York City," my mom exclaimed, pulling the flyer off the wall.

Runway?? I envisioned myself in front of a camera, striking poses, not the runway! And another problem?? It was at the same time as my German AP final exam. But anything is possible, I'm reminded.

So we go to the boutique store the next day with me wearing my mom's heels, and I fake knowing how to walk a runway—and crazily enough, book the gig!

My mom, the master of seeing through obstacles, then marches to my school principal and tells them I have been offered a unique "immersive cultural arts experience" and asks what is possible for the AP exam. In no time, I am granted an exemption to take the exam on a make-up date.

Both are possible.

Now fast forward to after the runway show. I am back at the hotel failing to wash out my massively teased hair from the show at midnight wondering if it would ever take its natural shape again with a huge smile thinking, *Wow, what is my life right now?* I am returning from modeling at 3 a.m. New Jersey time, only to be flying back across the country the next day to be back at school.

I returned to school a different person. My perspective was expanded, and I knew I could do more than I had previously allowed myself to imagine. Life changes when we allow ourselves to open to further solutions before immediately closing the door to the seemingly impossible.

And although I grew up with a role model who thought broadly, that doesn't mean I have always been able to think in that same manner. I have continually worked to expand my perspective and have found it is one of the most profound ways to reach a new mountain in life.

This month I share some of my favorite and most impactful lessons in expanding perspective. Inevitably leading to more joyful freedom.

SPREAD JOY!
Invite someone with different views to coffee and practice listening more than speaking.

THOUGHTS CREATE EMOTIONS

Change the way you look at things and the things you look at change.
—WAYNE DYER

Emotions don't appear out of nowhere—they are responses to our thoughts. Emotions are always valid, but thoughts are not always Truth. We must examine our thoughts to shift our emotional homes. If we tune inward, we will be able to recognize that we frequent a particular emotional home, like sadness or fear, which has been created from our current thought patterns becoming familiar— and maybe even comfortable.

What we feel is a direct result of what we believe. To feel better, we need to start thinking better.

REFLECTION

Notice your thoughts during moments of low energy or frustration. What story are you telling yourself?

_____

_____

_____

_____

What thought could you choose instead—one that feels lighter or more empowering? If you feel stuck on cultivating a different thought, sit with the question, *Is this story I am telling myself true?*

_____

_____

_____

_____

How do your emotions shift when your inner narrative shifts?

_____

_____

_____

_____

PRACTICE

Write down a list of the most common or difficult thoughts that came up for you this week.

Then, for each one, write a counter thought—a more uplifting, compassionate, or empowering way to view the same situation—to help shift your perspective. With consistent practice, you'll gradually align with more joyful, kind, and resilient responses instead of falling back into self-negating patterns.

Examples:

- *I am not enough. → I am already whole, worthy, and more than enough just as I am.*

- *If only I had more money. → I have everything I need today, and I embody abundance.*

- *My stomach looks big. → My body is strong, alive, and healthy— I appreciate it and care for it with kindness.*

- *I'm a failure. → I'm a learner, a grower, and someone who gets up every time I fall down.*

- *I should have done better. → I did the best I could with the knowledge and resources I had—I can celebrate my progress and learn from this.*

_____

_____

_____

_____

_____

_____

IMAGINE THE BEST-CASE SCENARIO

*What if everything you are going through
is preparing you for what you asked for?*
—UNKNOWN

We're often taught to plan for the worst—but what if, instead, we planned for the best? Shifting your perspective in this way opens the door for life to unfold in the direction you truly hope for. The mind is a storyteller and master manifestor; when you feed it uplifting stories, it begins to shape new possibilities. A miracle, after all, is simply a shift in perception—so what miracles might arise when you choose to see through this lens? And trust me—when these miracles unfold, you'll feel pure, unshakable joy.

REFLECTION
How often do you catch yourself focusing on what could go wrong? How often do you imagine what could go right?

_____

_____

_____

_____

Take a current situation in your life and say out loud: *What if the best possible outcome occurs?* How does it feel in your body and heart to consider this?

_____

_____

_____

_____

If you chose to focus more of your attention on these possibilities, how might that shift the results—or the joy you experience along the way?

_____

_____

_____

_____

PRACTICE

Choose one current situation in your life and imagine 5 fantastic outcomes that could unfold in this situation that you may not have acknowledged yet. Now choose the best possible outcome from these 5 based on your perspective and rewrite it with the most beautiful, joy-filled ending you can imagine. Be specific and use all the senses to describe how well the ending plays out.

SHIFT YOUR LANGUAGE, SHIFT YOUR LIFE

The words you speak become the house you live in.
—ḤĀFIẒ

Words shape your world. Even small shifts in language can transform your emotional experience. Every word you speak carries energy—it influences how you see the world and how you experience yourself. The vibration behind your words affects your emotions too. If you want to feel joy, the words you choose will powerfully determine whether you feel free or trapped, elated or weighed down, a creator or a follower.

REFLECTION

Which "I am" statements do you repeat consistently perhaps without even realizing it on autopilot? Are these creating what you want or what you don't want?

_____

_____

_____

_____

Do you ever catch yourself saying "I have to . . . "? How does it feel in your body when you say those words?

_____

_____

_____

_____

Can you recall a time when changing your words changed the way you felt— or even the outcome of a situation? If this is not coming to mind easily, can you reflect on a time where you regretted the words you said immediately— how did these shape your emotional tone?

_____

_____

_____

_____

PRACTICE

Replace *"I have to"* with *"I get to."*

Say it out loud and feel the shift.

Try this reframe in 5 real-life scenarios:

1. I get to _____

2. I get to _____

3. I get to _____

4. I get to _____

5. I get to _____

Notice what you place after I AM—two of the most powerful words you can use. (e.g., I am tired, I am behind, I am not good enough).

What do you now choose to declare instead? This is what you will create. (e.g., I am resilient, I am learning, I am limitless)

I am _____

I am _____

I am _____

I am _____

I am _____

I am _____

BONUS

Notice how the change from *I have to* to *I get to* affects your energy. Which task felt most transformed with this new perspective?

YOU ARE THE CREATOR

Obstacles don't block the path. They are the path.
—ZEN PROVERB

What if your challenges are actually sacred invitations? Every obstacle is an opportunity to deepen your strength, perspective, or purpose. In other words, what if everything the universe puts in front of you is for you—to learn to increase your frequency and lead with love?

This means everything you encounter and come across is intended for your eyes and for your transformational growth into joy.

REFLECTION
What current challenge are you facing? How might it be *for* you? What are you learning because of it?

_____

_____

_____

_____

What are you letting shift your mood that doesn't have to be an obstacle? *For example: Do you sway with the weather of the day, or wake up refreshed only to feel low after seeing the news?*

_____

_____

_____

_____

What would it look like to root your sense of peace and presence from within—regardless of whether the sun is shining or rain is falling, literally and figuratively?

_____

_____

_____

_____

What is one action you can take this week to start changing your reference point for joy regardless of the obstacles around you?

_____

_____

_____

_____

Tip: Referencing your inner world rather than external circumstances gives you your power back—and leads to a more sustainable sense of peace.

PRACTICE

Name a past obstacle that, in hindsight, helped you grow.

Write a gratitude letter to this obstacle!

BONUS

Think of a belief, pattern, or view you held at the start of this month. Notice if it shifted, widened, or softened. Write a single line beginning with *I now see that* . . . and let it capture the opening that occurred.

GRATITUDE PAGES

_____   _____

_____   _____

_____   _____

_____   _____

_____   _____

_____   _____

_____   _____

_____   _____

_____   _____

_____   _____

_____   _____

_____   _____

_____   _____

GRATITUDE PAGES

_____

_____

_____

_____

_____

_____

_____

_____

_____

_____

_____

_____

GRATITUDE PAGES

_____

_____

_____

_____

_____

_____

_____

_____

_____

_____

_____

TAKE RESPONSIBILITY

Argue for your limitations and, sure enough, they're yours.
—RICHARD BACH

One ordinary day, I caught myself worrying about how many people were signing up for a workshop I was teaching.

Would there be enough people to look like a solid group? Was there enough interest in the workshop? Had I marketed it properly?

My mind spun with thoughts until I realized how mundane this issue really was. Why was I giving it so much energy?

I had just overcome several more real obstacles: One that required legal advice. One that needed a permit approval to run my business. One that involved a family health issue. Obstacles that I would deem far more worthy of my worry.

And that's when it hit me: I did not currently have any real problems.

I had a house, food, a loving family, friends, a functioning business.

And yet—instead of feeling ecstatically at ease—my mind was still scanning for the next greatest threat.

This is the way of the mind—or rather, the way of the ego—always searching, always bracing for what could go wrong.

In that moment, I realized something profound: There will always be obstacles . . . always be stresses . . . always be problems to solve.

But I could become *consciously aware* of how I was perceiving each one.

And even more: I could choose to feel joy *while* moving through them. I could even choose to open my eyes and see that often . . . I didn't really have a "problem" at all.

Maybe I just had something to act on. Something to figure out.

But it didn't have to steal my peace.

I knew this logically long before, but in this moment it became a visceral knowing. That *aha* moment turned an ordinary day into an extraordinary one. I could take responsibility for deciding whether something truly required my "worry."

And I was ready to choose joy instead.

This month I hope the journey will lead to the realization that taking responsibility for every circumstance is taking back your power. When you are not the victim but the creator, then you are never helpless. Instead, you can take action to create your desired life.

SPREAD JOY!

Give your server or barista a generous tip and thank them sincerely.

WAKE UP TO YOUR POWER

You are the sky. Everything else—it's just the weather.
—PEMA CHÖDRÖN

True joy and freedom come when we stop blaming, stop controlling, and fully own our lives with compassion and integrity. That is power!

The first step to taking responsibility is noticing where we *give away* our power—to fear, to worry, to circumstances. Notice how often your mind creates problems when none truly exist. Realize you have a choice to choose joy.

REFLECTION
THREATS

Where are you scanning for threats that don't really exist? Is there a theme?

_____

_____

How often are you okay . . . but looking for something to fix or worry about? Were you taught that you should worry? Was this necessary when you were younger but not now?

_____

_____

_____

COMPLAINTS

What complaint are you ready to lay to rest? How much freedom would this provide you?

_____

_____

Does holding onto these complaints benefit you?

_____

_____

_____

PRACTICE

POWER DRAINING DETECTIVE

Spend one day noticing every time you catch yourself worrying, complaining, or feeling like a victim.

Jot it down without judgment: "Today I worried about _____. Today I complained about _____."

At the end of the day, ask: **Was this truly a problem, or just a thought?**

To create a physical shift, practice equal ratio breathing and count your inhale and exhale until they are both at a count of 5.

COMPASSIONATE RESPONSIBILITY

We must be conscious and responsible for our
beliefs and behaviors if we are ever to be free.
—BRENDON BURCHARD

Own how you participate in your reality—without blame or shame. Taking responsibility doesn't mean beating yourself up. It means asking: What decisions, patterns, or thoughts have I contributed? And what new choices can I make? When you do this, fear shifts to love, and everything in your path becomes a lesson guiding you toward your desires and values.

REFLECTION
How could you have compassionately contributed to your current challenges?

_____

_____

_____

_____

What opposing goals might you have? For example, wanting freedom but craving security or wanting to be thinner but craving sweets.

_____

_____

_____

_____

What decisions or patterns am I ready to shift?

_____

_____

_____

_____

What would your mood be if you won the lottery today? Are you waiting for someone to hand you joy? How can you choose to feel the same elation of winning the lottery in the present amongst your perceived challenges?

_____

_____

_____

_____

PRACTICE
OBSTACLE INQUIRY
Pick one conflict or obstacle you're facing.

Ask yourself:

- How have I contributed to this situation?
- What choices have led me here?
- Where can I choose differently now?
- Write about it *as if you are your own best friend.*

PLAYFUL TRUST

Surrender to what is. Let go of what was. Have faith in what will be.
—SONIA RICOTTI

Lighten up and let go of control. Life is meant to be played with, not fought against. When you cling to outcomes, you limit yourself to what's familiar—and often miss the best possibilities. By loosening your grip, you open the door to flow, ease, and joy—and allow miracles to unfold. First, take responsibility for how your need to control limits your experiences. Then, invite playful trust into your life.

My dad always said, "Go play and learn!" when he dropped me off at school. This week, take his advice: Go play and learn—and simply see what unfolds.

REFLECTION
Where might you be gripping so tightly to outcomes that you leave little to no room for trust?

_____

_____

_____

_____

How does it feel to loosen your grip just a little bit—to step back and let the universe lead?

_____

_____

_____

_____

How can you invite more playfulness into your week?

_____

_____

_____

_____

Do you find it easier to learn when you allow yourself to play in the process?

_____

_____

_____

_____

PRACTICE
CONTROL SURRENDER
Pick one small area of your life where you're overcontrolling (ex: your partner's habits, your business success, your appearance).

- Consciously surrender this for one week.

- Replace control with *play*:

- What's a creative and fun next step I can take with complete curiosity of the outcome? What if you viewed this obstacle as the game of life? Would it feel different?

- What if you improvised with each step?

LIVE IN INTEGRITY

You must take personal responsibility. You cannot change the circumstances,
the seasons, or the wind, but you can change yourself.
—JIM ROHN

Align your thoughts, words, and actions. This is where real freedom and contentment are born because when we live in integrity of what we said we were going to do, we stand taller and feel prouder of ourselves.

True responsibility means living from your inner truth—saying what you mean, doing what you say, and thinking thoughts that uplift your path.

REFLECTION

Where are your thoughts, words, and actions not matching?

_____

_____

_____

_____

How does it feel when you say yes to something but your thoughts and actions are saying no?

_____

_____

_____

How would it feel to live even 5 percent more aligned this week?

_____

_____

_____

What is one small shift toward greater integrity that you can make today?

_____

_____

_____

PRACTICE
INTEGRITY AUDIT

Notice where you are out of alignment. Are you saying yes when you mean no, thinking from scarcity but talking abundance, or saying I can't when you really can?

When you catch yourself saying *I can't*, pause and flip the internal dialogue to *I am willing* or *I am not willing*. This is taking responsibility for your life and being honest about whether something is a priority.

You can't make it to the gym or you are not willing to prioritize that over other tasks? You can't go to the event you'd enjoy because your spouse wants to spend time together or you are not willing to tell your spouse what you really want?

I can't _____

    I am willing _____ or

    I am not willing_____

I can't _____

    I am willing _____ or

    I am not willing_____

I can't _____

    I am willing _____ or

    I am not willing_____

BONUS

Sit quietly and place your hands gently over your heart. Reflect on your relationship with responsibility—how has it shifted for you this month? Notice the ways stepping into your power has brought you more freedom.

Breathe deeply and ask yourself: What old complaint, controlling thought, or victim story am I ready to release forever? Write down whatever arises, without judgment. Feel the weight lift as you let it go.

GRATITUDE PAGES

GRATITUDE PAGES

_____

_____

_____

_____

_____

_____

_____

_____

_____

_____

_____

_____

GRATITUDE PAGES

_____   _____

_____   _____

_____   _____

_____   _____

_____   _____

_____   _____

_____   _____

_____   _____

_____   _____

_____   _____

_____   _____

_____   _____

INVEST IN YOURSELF

When you take care of yourself, you're a better human for others.
You give more, serve more, love more.
—KRIS CARR

I arrived at the studio on Monday night, filled with that familiar excitement to teach yoga—not anticipating what I'd find on the other side of the door.

What I walked into was . . . a mess. Grey, crumbly muck was scattered across the floor, buried in the crevices of the radiator, and—of course on the first day I left them out—dusting my singing bowls.

I looked up. Drip. Drip. Drip.

A pipe was leaking from the ceiling where a tile had collapsed, and the steady rhythm of water hitting the floor felt less like a soothing sound bath and more like a tiny percussive panic attack.

Cue my past life in oil and gas. All the safety training started speaking up. *What is in this pipe? Could there be asbestos in the ceiling? Do I have the proper equipment to clean this up?*

I briskly marched down the stairs to the property manager, rehearsing my concerns in my head. Her response was very different from mine. She strolled upstairs, scooped the grey gunk up with bare hands, and calmly said, "It's just water."

I wasn't entirely convinced, but I nodded like I believed her.

Maybe my manufacturing experience had caused me to be more cautious than necessary.

Together we got the worst of it cleaned and set up trash cans under the leak when my private client arrived—miraculously late, giving us just enough time to manage the situation.

Before she left, I asked if the building's cleaning crew could handle the rest before my group class at 6:30. She said yes. Relief washed over me.

Until 6:00.

One student showed up, but no cleaning crew.

6:10—still nothing. I couldn't wait anymore.

Determined to handle this myself, I bent down to grab my handheld vacuum. That's when I heard *BANG*. Not just any sound—*my head* colliding with the sharp metal bracket holding up the Wi-Fi router.

It was one of those surreal moments where I heard the noise before I even felt the pain.

The one student present popped into the kitchenette, "Are you okay?" Pause. "Oh . . . you're bleeding."

I touched my forehead trying to gauge the seriousness.

"I think you should go to the bathroom to look at it," he suggested gently.

I looked in the mirror, surprised. This was not a small cut—it was a full-blown *gash*.

Just then, in rolled the cleaning crew. Of course! Two minutes more patience and I could've avoided my forehead situation entirely.

Back in the studio, I fumbled for the first aid kit. Thankfully, my student used to be a firefighter and stepped in to help, but the location of the wound made bandaging awkward, so I pressed gauze to it until the bleeding stopped.

But no more time to dwell. It was 6:30. Class time.

I grounded my feet, took a deep breath, and repeated the mantra my teacher taught me:

How may I serve?

And then—just like that—it was time to serve.

After class, the one student who witnessed everything looked at me and said, "I don't know how you stayed calm and just *taught* after that. I'm truly impressed."

I smiled. "It's the yoga."

But more than that—it was the thousands of hours I've spent learning how to regulate stress, digest emotions, and meet the moment with presence through my yoga training. It was all the time, energy, and money I've invested in myself that gave me the tools to show up—not perfectly, but fully.

Sometimes we think investing in ourselves is optional.

But when life drips uncertainty from the ceiling and it hits you in the forehead, you'll be glad you did.

Please don't wait for a special occasion or reason to invest in yourself. It is always the perfect time. The time is now—this month to be exact!

SPREAD JOY!

Pay it forward by buying the coffee (or toll, or parking meter) for the car or person behind you.

REMEMBER YOUR WORTH

To love oneself is the beginning of a lifelong romance.
—OSCAR WILDE

You are the most valuable investment you'll ever make. We often spend more time and money on our homes, our cars, or even fleeting pleasures, than we do on the one place we'll live forever—our body and soul. Belongings may come and go, but you will always still be in your body, whether it's feeling vibrant from attention or painful from neglect.

You are not a side character. You are the main character in your story. Treat yourself like it. Your health and happiness is the greatest return on investment that exists!

REFLECTION

If you truly believed you were your most valuable asset, how would that shift the way you spend your time and energy?

_____

_____

_____

_____

Where have you been underinvesting in yourself? Where do you want to start investing more in yourself through money, time, or energy?

_____

_____

_____

_____

PRACTICE
TAKE INVENTORY

Where does your time, energy, and money go—do you know the top 3 areas? What does that reveal about your priorities?

Are those priorities aligned with the values you chose in Month 4? What would the top 3 areas be to spend your time, energy, and money based on that month's answers?

What is one thing you can invest in that supports your Month 4 heart desires?

Choose *one* area—body, mind, or soul—and do something nourishing that supports its longevity.

Mind Shift: *I am worth the time, care, and energy it takes to thrive.*

TRUE SELF-CARE VS. NUMBING OUT

Self-care is not a luxury. It's a necessity.
—AUDRE LORDE

Self-care isn't always luxurious or social. It's sometimes saying no, going to therapy, drinking water, sitting still in meditation, doing the thing you've been avoiding. Wine, movie nights, and shopping sprees may offer a fun, quick fix— but deep care truly heals, is sustainable, and provides you more energy to do what you want. And when you have the energy to fulfill your desires, joy will be so much easier to feel and access.

REFLECTION

When do you skip self-care, claiming you're too tired, even though it would refresh your body and feed your soul?

_____

_____

_____

_____

What would self-care look like if you based it on what you truly need rather than what's convenient or popular?

_____

_____

_____

_____

What would you do differently if you wanted to feel good *long after* the moment?

_____

_____

_____

_____

PRACTICE

Look at your current self-care practices. Make a list of which ones *nourish* you long-term and which ones just distract or numb?

Replace one surface-level treat with something that deeply restores your nervous system or supports your goals, such as:

- *Yoga class to release tension*
- *Meditation to calm your mind*
- *Meaningful time with a friend to nourish your heart*
- *Mentorship program to grow toward your goals*
- *Practice Yoga Nidra to restore deep rest*

Yoga Nidra is one of the most powerful healing tools—and yet it's often overlooked because it seems too simple. But don't let simplicity fool you: Its effects are profound. Research shows it can be even more restorative than sleep, while gently bringing subconscious thoughts to the surface so you can heal what you may not be aware of.

You can find free recordings on YouTube, Spotify, or on my Insight Timer profile. The more consistently you practice Yoga Nidra, the more energy, clarity, and creativity you'll cultivate. Never underestimate its transformative power.

MAKE THE INVESTMENT

If you don't make time for your wellness,
you'll be forced to make time for your illness.
—JOYCE SUNADA

Don't wait until retirement, the next vacation, or after you "earn it." Joy, vitality, and purpose are not delayed rewards. They are meant to be felt in the present moment. One of my coworkers used to constantly talk, and honestly brag, about how he had millions saved for retirement. Then, sadly, he had a fatal heart attack just weeks before retirement. It was devastating to witness, and I know there are many similar stories too. You are worthy of investing in what you need now before a large life milestone.

Please don't postpone living.

REFLECTION
What have you been waiting for the "right time" to do?

_____

_____

_____

_____

What would your life look like if you gave yourself permission to enjoy it now?

_____

_____

_____

_____

PRACTICE

Choose *one thing* you've been putting off for "someday"—and begin today. It could be a class, a health routine, a yoga training, or a creative pursuit.

Treat it like a real investment—because it is. Here's how:

1. **Commit your time and energy:** Schedule it in your calendar as you would a meeting or appointment.
2. **Allocate resources:** Invest money, tools, or materials needed to support your growth.
3. **Show up consistently:** Small, regular steps compound over time, just like financial investments. Remember that everything is energy—time and money.
4. **Track progress:** Notice improvements, insights, or breakthroughs along the way—celebrate them.
5. **Prioritize it:** Treat it as nonnegotiable. Protect the time and energy you dedicate to it.

SURROUND YOURSELF WITH EXPANDERS

You are the average of the five people you spend the most time with.
—JIM ROHN

One of the greatest investments you can make is seeking out mentors, teachers, and communities that elevate you. If you're the smartest or most grounded person in the room, you're in the wrong room. To inspire joy, find someone with your best interest at heart who can guide you through the ups and downs and toward your life dreams.

REFLECTION
Who in your life helps you grow? Who might you need to spend less time with to make space for people who elevate you?

_____

_____

_____

_____

How might you need to do research or get out into the world to meet a mentor(s) that can guide you toward your highest self?

_____

_____

_____

_____

If you are not sure, simply setting the intention that you seek a mentor is a great first step which will start to lead you toward the mentor that is right for you. As is said in yoga, when the student is ready, the teacher will appear.

_____

_____

_____

_____

PRACTICE

Identify one or two people whose energy, values, or life path you admire.

Learn from them: read their work, reach out for coffee, take their course, or ask a bold question. Making this connection and expanding your understanding of what is possible in life will bring immense joy. Watch what happens when you do this over and over!

BONUS

Place one hand over your belly and one over your heart. Breathe into the ways you nourished yourself this month—through time, care, or energy. Write one sentence that completes this thought: *When I invest in myself, I . . .*

GRATITUDE PAGES

_____   _____

_____   _____

_____   _____

_____   _____

_____   _____

_____   _____

_____   _____

_____   _____

_____   _____

_____   _____

_____   _____

_____   _____

GRATITUDE PAGES

_____   _____

_____   _____

_____   _____

_____   _____

_____   _____

_____   _____

_____   _____

_____   _____

_____   _____

_____   _____

_____   _____

_____   _____

GRATITUDE PAGES

_____

_____

_____

_____

_____

_____

_____

_____

_____

_____

_____

_____

CREATE FROM YOUR PURPOSE

No matter how small you start, start something that matters.
—BRENDON BURCHARD

An errand brought me to the other side of town—a place I rarely visit—and I found myself stuck in traffic as high schoolers crossed the street, buzzing with the freedom of their school day's end. As I waited for the backup to clear, something caught my eye: a small, painted sign hanging on a utility pole. In bold, colorful letters, it read: **EMPATHY**.

My heart lifted. I had finally seen one in person! I'd heard about the Empathy Sign Project and glimpsed it online—a grassroots initiative by someone who hand-paints EMPATHY signs and hangs them randomly around town. Their mission: to spread empathy, one sign at a time. But until now, I had never encountered one in real life.

Just the thought of someone creating these messages and placing them quietly around the city, with no attachment, moved me. It was such a simple yet powerful act—offering art in service of the heart—which in turn uplifted mine.

That moment reminded me of the powerful influence that happens when we create from purpose. When we express ourselves to uplift, heal, and connect with others, guided by our inner callings, the impact is immediate and lasting—contributing to others even if we never meet the people we reach.

When I reflect on my own journey, I realize I've always been happiest when I was creating from that place. Whether I was painting, baking, playing the piano, experimenting with makeup while modeling, or designing products in engineering—every activity I was drawn to involved some form of creation. At the time, it may have seemed like I was chasing a wide range of interests, but now I see the common thread: I was passionate about the act of bringing an idea into form.

Each creative outlet gave me a sense of aliveness and expression. I could lose myself for hours in the flow of making, shaping, building.

But something shifted when I began creating with clear purpose. It wasn't just about self-expression anymore—it became about contribution. I discovered that our impulse to create is universal, even sacred, and when we direct it toward something meaningful, it becomes transformative.

That's why yoga became so central to my life. Of all the things I've created, teaching yoga aligned most deeply with my heart. I remember a class when a student came up afterwards with tears in her eyes, and said, "This is the first time I have felt peace all year." I hadn't done anything specifically for her situation—I simply held space, created safety, and let yoga do its magic. I could see how teaching yoga is practicing something greater than myself that helps us all transform from the inside out.

Creating from purpose became the bridge between joy and service. It revealed not only what I could do—but who I really was.

I believe that when we create from purpose, we return to joy. We remember our power, our humanity, and our connection to something greater.

You'll have a chance to work with questions like the ones below this month to connect to your bigger picture and enjoy the process:

- *When have I felt most aligned, alive, or in flow while creating something?*
- *What deeper value, belief, or intention was guiding me in that moment?*
- *How can I bring more of that into what I'm creating now?*

SPREAD JOY!

Send a handwritten letter or card to someone who wouldn't expect it.

REMEMBER WHAT MOVES YOU

*Follow your bliss and the universe will open doors
where there were only walls.*
—JOSEPH CAMPBELL

Reconnect with the spark that's always been there.

Purpose often lives in the moments when we feel most alive—not in a title or role, but in a felt experience. Oftentimes it requires us to let go of prestige or what might externally seem most impressive. Your heart, in a whisper or fiery passion, will guide you to your true purpose.

Spend time on these to dig deep because sometimes the heart speaks in the faintest of whispers!

PRACTICE
Reflect on your childhood joys, peak life moments, and recurring passions.

Write down every one of these memories that comes to mind.

Add every detail of how you felt that you can recall. Notice how it feels in your body. Sit in a peaceful place and allow the feeling to settle and fully absorb into your being. Once you have reveled in this expanded sense of peace, move on to the reflection questions.

REFLECTION

During these moments, what were you doing, and what need were you meeting? Are there any themes among them?

_____

_____

_____

_____

What did these moments teach you about what you care most deeply about?

_____

_____

_____

_____

TUNE INWARD, TURN DOWN THE NOISE

Your vision will become clear only when you can look into your own heart. Who looks outside, dreams; who looks inside, awakes.
—CARL JUNG

Purpose isn't usually shouted; it's heard in bored moments of space between activities or even a friend telling us when they saw us smile when our inner voice was too quiet for us to hear. We must slow down and listen if we want a chance to follow our call.

The heart speaks more softly than the mind, but its wisdom runs deeper. We connect with joy when we align with the voice of our true purpose.

PRACTICE

Try a daily stillness practice to tune into your inner voice. A few options are provided for you:

- Naming your breath meditation: On the inhale say to yourself *breathing in*, on the exhale say to yourself *breathing out*

- Slow walks: Take a walk while holding this question in mind, *What does my purpose want to express today?*

- Time in nature: Lie down fully in the grass or find a place to sit at the base of a tree. Close your eyes, feel the sun or breeze on your skin and listen to the sounds of nature.

- Afterward ask yourself: What does my heart want? What would it want me to know?

- Write down what arises. It may take several practices for you to hear what is there for you. Your heart may not speak in words but an emotion, physical sensation, or simply a knowing.

REFLECTION

If you stripped away the "shoulds" and expectations of others, what would you feel joyful to create?

_____

_____

_____

_____

Look back at Month 4, Clarify Your Heart's Desires. What insight does this provide? Has anything changed?

_____

_____

_____

_____

CREATE WITH PLAYFULNESS

Almost all creativity requires purposeful play.
—ABRAHAM MASLOW

What matters is not how "good" it is—but how *alive* it makes you feel. Play is not a luxury—it's a form of self-expression and inner connection. Children don't ask if they're good at playing, they just do it. Let's remember that freedom. When innocent creativity is fueled by purpose, it becomes a force of service, healing, and impact.

PRACTICE
Carve out one nonnegotiable hour in your weekly schedule for unstructured play—doodle, dance in your room, build something, collage, visit an art museum, sing out loud.

Choose a creative outlet that brings value to your well-being.

REFLECTION

Recall the last time you truly felt playful—what made it so freeing?

_____

_____

_____

_____

What beliefs or barriers hold you back from feeling playful? How might you acknowledge them with compassion and invite more childlike curiosity, wonder, and freedom into your daily life?

_____

_____

_____

_____

Food for Thought: If you are feeling stuck creatively in any way, how can you learn something new? Look for classes where you can learn a new skill and watch how your life opens up to new ideas and possibilities!

EMBODY THE CREATOR WITHIN

You are not a drop in the ocean. You are the entire ocean in a drop.
—RUMI

You are already a creator. It is time for you to own this truth. Your life is your canvas, and every choice is an act of creation. Even your thoughts, words, and boundaries are strokes of your creative truth. You are always manifesting with every action you take, whether you know it or not. The more intentional your actions, the more you will find your dream life emerges.

PRACTICE

Every morning, before you start your day, take 5 deep breaths and repeat to yourself:

I am a creator. My intentions bring my world into form.

Let this be your creative anchor this week and consider one intentional action you can take each day to align with your highest expression of creativity.

Create a list of your top 5 most creative desires.

1. _____

2. _____

3. _____

4. _____

5. _____

What is one small, realistic action you can take this week to bring each to fruition? Without action these will always remain dreams.

Start every project with a purpose ritual—a moment to connect with your creativity and remember that you are a creator, guided by a higher purpose.

    Some purpose-ritual ideas: light a favorite candle, choose a playlist that helps you ease into your creative flow, or pause at the threshold of your creative space, take a deep breath, and bow in reverence before entering.

REFLECTION
Is there any energetic shift you need to make in order to attract these heartfelt desires into your life?

    For example:

- Shifting from self-doubt to self-trust.
- Replacing overcommitment with healthy boundaries.
- Moving from fear of speaking up to using your authentic voice.
- Choosing gratitude instead of focusing on what's missing.

_____

_____

_____

_____

BONUS

Close your eyes and remember one moment when you felt lit up by purpose. Notice how your body responds as you revisit it. Write a phrase beginning with *My purpose creates . . .* to remind you of what flows from living aligned.

GRATITUDE PAGES

_____   _____

_____   _____

_____   _____

_____   _____

_____   _____

_____   _____

_____   _____

_____   _____

_____   _____

_____   _____

_____   _____

_____   _____

GRATITUDE PAGES

_____   _____

_____   _____

_____   _____

_____   _____

_____   _____

_____   _____

_____   _____

_____   _____

_____   _____

_____   _____

_____   _____

_____   _____

GRATITUDE PAGES

_____   _____

_____   _____

_____   _____

_____   _____

_____   _____

_____   _____

_____   _____

_____   _____

_____   _____

_____   _____

_____   _____

_____   _____

SPEAK YOUR TRUTH

Speak your truth, even if your voice shakes.
—MAGGIE KUHN

I can still hear Oprah's voice telling a reporter that there's one question nearly everyone asks her after she interviews them. After conducting thousands of interviews from politicians, pop stars, humanitarians, and parents—everyone still asks the same thing once the cameras cut:

"Was that okay?"

Even high profile celebrities, those who've spoken on the biggest stages and held the world's attention for decades, ask it. It's the quiet plea underneath our boldest expressions: *Was I enough? Did you see me? Did it land?*

No matter who we are, at the end of the day, we all desire to be **seen, heard, and loved**.

I haven't had the chance to be interviewed by Oprah yet (though for the record, I'm ready and it would be an honor), but her words echoed in my mind when I realized that I had continuously been asking myself this question—after teaching yoga workshops or providing advice to a student going through a tragic life event, for example. And the question only ramped up in intensity after publishing my memoir *The Year of Sarah*. I'd been asking myself the same question in different forms—again and again.

Not out loud. But in my body. In the moments right after . . .

. . . leaving a Women's Wisdom Circle where I had shared vulnerably.

. . . finishing a podcast interview.

. . . someone messaging me that they'd read the book.

. . . opening up one-on-one about a story that had never seen the light of day.

In those quiet moments after, I would feel it stir:

"Was that okay?"

When I stayed stuck in "Was that okay?" I often felt a tightening in my chest, a restless replay in my mind, and a hollow fatigue in my body—like I had handed my power over for someone else to decide my worth. But when I allowed myself to ask, "Was that real? Was that honest?" something shifted. My breath softened. Joy bubbled up quietly, like a deep exhale. Even if my words weren't polished, I felt a steadiness, a kind of inner freedom that no outside approval could give me. That joy was proof that authenticity, not perfection, is what truly nourishes us.

And then I noticed something even more subtle:

That same question was also there *before* I spoke.

"Will this be okay?"

Will this message be helpful? Will it trigger someone? Will it be misunderstood? Will it change how they see me?

The ante rises every time you speak your truth. Especially when that truth is no longer whispered in the safety of small groups, but printed and published for the world to see. There's a new level of exposure—and with it, new vulnerability.

And let's be honest: Telling the truth can be disruptive.

It can strike open wounds. It can stir grief or spark anger.

It can challenge narratives that feel safe.

This guidebook could have caused some of this already for you too!

And I think this question beforehand can cause many of us to withdraw from speaking. When we focus on the potential for ruffling feathers and we're not carefully aware of this, **we confuse peacekeeping with truth avoiding**. Yet the world needs to hear our Truths. We are not meant to hide, and everyone has something valuable to share.

The only way to expand into who we're meant to be is to get more and more honest with ourselves—and the world. To speak what's real, even when our voices shake. To show up, even if our knees knock. Until then, we will only be suppressing what is in our hearts.

Because in the end, speaking our truth isn't about getting it perfect. It's about being real. It's about choosing authenticity over approval. And maybe, slowly, we begin to ask a different question.

Not "Was that okay?"

But:

Was that real?

Was that honest?

Was that true to who I am?

And if the answer is yes—then it was more than okay.

It was powerful. It was brave.

It was necessary.

And if the answer is no—make an apology.

It is okay to ask for forgiveness.

It is okay to admit mistakes.

You can be proud that you had the courage to stay true to you. You can relish in the joy that you did the hard thing. You can sleep well at night, knowing you did your very best from a deep well of love.

This month, let your voice be heard!

SPREAD JOY!

Text someone just to say "I'm grateful for you" or "I'm thinking of you."

THE COURAGE TO BE SEEN

To share your weakness is to make yourself vulnerable; to make yourself vulnerable is to show your strength.
—CRISS JAMI

Keeping our voice silent causes emotions to stay stuck or lodged in our body. Over time this will create a weight that ties down our joy.

We all crave to be seen, understood, and loved—but that can only happen when we're willing to show who we truly are. Speaking your truth begins with allowing vulnerability, which is the gateway to authentic connection.

PRACTICE

Share one vulnerable truth with someone safe—something you've been holding back, even if it's small.

Bonus: practice this twice this week!

Send a short voice message to someone you've been wanting to reach out to—whether it's to share something from your heart, offer appreciation, or make a request you've been holding back. Speaking out loud allows your true voice and energy to be felt, carrying tone and warmth that written words sometimes lose.

REFLECTION
When do you feel most authentic when speaking?

_____

_____

_____

_____

Are you willing to let your words be messy as you learn to use your voice?

_____

_____

_____

_____

Mantra

My truth is worthy of being heard.

ASK BOLDLY, RECEIVE FULLY

You get in life what you have the courage to ask for.
—OPRAH WINFREY

We often deny ourselves the chance to receive because we don't speak up. Asking is not a burden—it's a bridge to connection, clarity, and care. People cannot read our minds to know what we want, and I have found that promotions, opportunities, or invitations are mostly granted to those who asked for them.

What is the worst that can happen? They say no, and you are right where you are now?

PRACTICE

Ask for one small thing today—support, space, a hug, feedback, help.

Pay attention to what gets in the way—guilt, fear of rejection, pride, or even the belief that your needs don't matter. Where do you feel that in your body? Is it a tightness in your chest, a knot in your stomach, a heaviness in your shoulders? Gently breathe into that space and acknowledge it with compassion. Then remind yourself: asking for what you need is not selfish—it's an act of kindness. Yes, actually kindness! Without it, you leave the other person guessing; with it, you invite connection and honesty.

REFLECTION

What is something you want or need that you've been afraid to ask for?

_____

_____

_____

_____

What would asking free up for you emotionally and energetically?

_____

_____

_____

_____

Mantra

I honor my needs and ask with confidence.

BOUNDARIES ARE LOVE

Daring to set boundaries is about having the courage to love ourselves even when we risk disappointing others.
—BRENÉ BROWN

Boundaries protect your joy. They're not walls but wise guidelines that teach others how to love and respect you—and how you love and respect yourself.

You teach others in every given moment how to treat you. If you feel someone is mistreating you, reflect on what you have allowed and likely a boundary needs to be created. You create joy in your life when you establish the guidelines on how you are to be treated.

PRACTICE

Name one boundary you need to set and name one boundary you created that you've outgrown.

Communicate one boundary with calm and clarity.

Hot Tip: No is a full sentence.

REFLECTION

Where in your life do you feel drained or resentful?

_____

_____

_____

_____

What boundary would shift that dynamic? Is this boundary needed with another and/or yourself?

_____

_____

_____

_____

Mantra

My boundaries are an act of self-love.

SAY THE THING

The truth will set you free, but first it will piss you off.
—GLORIA STEINEM

Truth telling can stir discomfort—both yours and others'. Yet honesty, when rooted in love, is liberating. Your words carry power. To become your healthiest, most joyful self, you must speak what needs to be spoken. At first, it may tumble out messy, but that's part of the process—the first step toward clearing space for joy. With practice, your truth will flow with more ease, and each time you speak it, the path becomes lighter.

PRACTICE

Say something honest and kind you've been holding in: a compliment, a thank-you, a heartfelt truth.

Notice what happens when you speak from clarity and love—not fear.

REFLECTION

What truth have you avoided sharing because you feared it would upset someone?

_____

_____

_____

_____

How might you express it with compassion?

_____

_____

_____

_____

Mantra

My truth heals, connects, and creates change.

BONUS

Close your eyes and notice if anything in this guidebook has stirred discomfort or resistance within you. Instead of pushing it away, gently ask yourself: *What is this trigger showing me about my growth edge in expressing myself?* Write one line that begins, *Speaking my truth means . . .* and allow it to be honest, even if it feels tender.

GRATITUDE PAGES

GRATITUDE PAGES

_____ _____

_____ _____

_____ _____

_____ _____

_____ _____

_____ _____

_____ _____

_____ _____

_____ _____

_____ _____

_____ _____

_____ _____

GRATITUDE PAGES

CREATE LIFE CHANGES

Change is not something that we should fear. Rather, it is something that we should welcome. For without change, nothing in this world would ever grow or blossom.

—B. K. S. IYENGAR

We're not meant to run from every challenge in life—but sometimes, change is exactly what's needed.

My junior year of college, I signed up for Philosophy 101. My husband (then boyfriend) and a few friends had taken it the previous semester and breezed through. "Super easy A," they said. "You'll love it!" they said.

Sold. I enrolled, dreaming of casual deep thoughts, easy grades, and meaningful metaphysical debates while sipping hot tea.

Two weeks in, I turned in my first paper—and got a C. Oof. Okay, not the end of the world, but I needed to bring that up. I poured even more of my heart into the second paper. B minus.

Improving, okay! But then my grades never went up from there.

The feedback? "Your reasoning is not logical."

What???

The class itself wasn't exactly a beacon of logic in my opinion. One lecture explored a thought experiment: *If you transplant someone's brain, are they still the same person?* Somehow, this spiraled into a conclusion that aliens *must* exist.

Meanwhile, my "out there" reflections were apparently *too* out there. My head spun with questions, none of which I could seem to answer correctly. Even my love tried to show me how my proofs weren't logically sound, but it just wasn't clicking.

Halfway through the semester, people gently suggested I drop the class. The teacher's assistant assured me a B was the best I could achieve at this point and getting a B isn't bad, but why let an elective jeopardize the GPA I'd worked so hard for in chemical engineering? This was supposed to be an easy A. Still, dropping felt like failure, and I mean *failure*. I was supposed to be good at deep thinking! I liked big questions! How could I not understand Philosophy 101?

At the final hour, I dropped the class. It was one of the only things I had ever quit in my life. I questioned myself. I obsessed over what I missed, mentally still not letting go as if that would enable me to understand what had just happened.

Now with more space from that moment, I see that course taught me a lesson I deeply needed: Sometimes the wisest move isn't pushing through— it's walking away.

Letting go of what's not working doesn't make you a quitter or a failure. It makes you someone who aligns with the priorities in their life. Letting go frees your energy to focus on what matters for your journey and for me that was not Philosophy 101. And that, I've come to learn, is its own kind of logic.

This month you'll strengthen the ability to set yourself free—reducing the elements of your life that are blocking joy from arising.

SPREAD JOY!

Donate one quality item you no longer need, creating space for something new in your life while helping another.

THE NATURE OF CHANGE

When patterns are broken, new worlds emerge.
—TULI KUPFERBERG

Change is inevitable. It's the current of life. A natural law. Yet, so often, we resist it—clinging to what is familiar even when it no longer serves us. Why? Because the unknown feels threatening. But what if the unknown holds a possibility better than we could imagine? Like the seasons, our lives are meant to evolve. Fighting change is like trying to hold back spring . . . it depletes joy.

PRACTICE

Reflect on a recent change in your life—big or small—and write in a stream of consciousness. Give yourself at least three pages. Often it is in the later thoughts that hidden truths begin to surface. Consider: What shifted for you? How did it affect your daily rhythm, emotions, or perspective? What was your initial reaction, and what do you notice now as you look back?

Anytime you are triggered by change this month, ask yourself this question:

- ***What if this is happening for me, not to me?***
- How do situations shift when you ask: What if this is happening for me, not to me?

REFLECTION

Do you want to grow and evolve? Ask yourself this honestly. There may be places you do and don't.

_____

_____

_____

_____

What change are you currently resisting? What would happen if you stopped fighting a certain change that is arising? What is trying to occur?

_____

_____

_____

_____

Mantra

I trust the rhythm of life and the seasons within me.

SMALL SHIFTS, BIG IMPACT

Small hinges swing big doors.
—W. CLEMENT STONE

A friend once told me about a trash can in her kitchen that lived inside a low cabinet. Every time she needed it, she had to stoop down and tug open the door—an annoying little ritual she repeated every day for years. One day, it occurred to her: *What if I just moved the can?* She did, and instantly released herself from a daily source of friction.

For me, it was switching my phone to silent. That tiny shift freed me from the nonstop interruption of pings and buzzes. These small, intentional choices—what seem like microdecisions—can gently recalibrate our nervous systems and invite more ease into our lives.

PRACTICE

What small, irritating thing have you been tolerating for too long? Choose one—and change it!

Try silencing your phone and turning off notifications for a full day. Notice the difference in your peace of mind.

Constant alerts pull our attention away from what matters, scattering our focus and reducing joy. Social media notifications can lure us into scrolling, creating an endless loop of shifting emotions that drains energy and fuels addictive cycles. By stepping away, you free yourself to direct your energy toward what you truly desire—living with clarity, calm, and intention.

REFLECTION

What other small daily discomforts are you tolerating that you could easily change?

_____

_____

_____

_____

What one shift could simplify your life right now?

_____

_____

_____

_____

Mantra

I deserve to release what no longer serves me, no matter how small.

INITIATING THE BIGGER CHANGE

*Change happens when the pain of staying the same
is greater than the pain of change.*
—TONY ROBBINS

There are times when life nudges us toward major change—new jobs, endings of relationships, shifts in identity. Some of these we resist until our body, emotions, or circumstances force us to listen. Not every discomfort calls for drastic change—but discernment can help us hear when it's time to act. This could be the difference between building frustration or joy.

PRACTICE

Think of a situation you're "pushing through." Are you starting to feel heavy, fatigued, helpless? Consider if this situation is calling on you to surrender or make a shift?

Is your body asking for a shift through signals of heartburn, bloating, acne, chronic coughing, etc. If your body could speak, what change would it ask for?

REFLECTION

Where in your life are you avoiding discomfort that might actually be a doorway to freedom?

_____

_____

_____

_____

What change are you scared to make, and what fear is underneath that? Ask yourself:

- Do I want to grow?
- Do I want to evolve?
- Do I really desire what I said I do?
- Am I choosing comfort over positive change?

_____

_____

_____

_____

Based on these answers, do you need to make a change or consciously choose to stay where you are and own that decision?

_____

_____

_____

Is it a situational change or perspective shift that you are most needing now?

_____

_____

_____

If it is a perspective shift, revisit Month 5 to release yourself from this pattern.

_____

_____

_____

Mantra

I release fear and welcome the transformation I am ready for.

LETTING GO AND MOVING FORWARD

In the process of letting go, you will lose many things from the past,
but you will find yourself.
—DEEPAK CHOPRA

Change often requires letting go—of habits, people-pleasing, outdated patterns, or roles we've outgrown. Sometimes, grief comes with this process, even when the change is positive. Letting go creates space for something new to bloom. You are not who you were—and that is beautiful.

PRACTICE

Identify one pattern, relationship, or behavior that no longer fits—and name it out loud. This could be as simple as having three coffees a day or more complex like constantly arguing over weekend plans with a partner.

Create a personal ritual to honor what you're releasing (write it down, burn it, plant it, etc.).

As you let something go, whisper "Thank you for how you served me and now I let you go" before releasing it. This brings a spirit of appreciation and acknowledgment to the letting-go process. If it is in your life, it supported you somehow at one time and that deserves gratitude.

REFLECTION

What are you still holding onto that is holding you back?

_____

_____

_____

_____

Who are you without this old story or pattern? Is it a more authentic you?

_____

_____

_____

_____

Mantra

I let go of what no longer serves me and welcome who I'm becoming.

BONUS

Take a breath and acknowledge one shift you made this month—big or small—that moved you closer to the life you want. Write one line beginning with *This change is teaching me . . .*

GRATITUDE PAGES

GRATITUDE PAGES

_____   _____

_____   _____

_____   _____

_____   _____

_____   _____

_____   _____

_____   _____

_____   _____

_____   _____

_____   _____

_____   _____

_____   _____

GRATITUDE PAGES

AUTHENTICALLY CONNECT

Joy is a net of love by which you can catch souls.
—MOTHER TERESA

One Christmas in Japan, I found myself wandering the streets of Takarazuka with no destination in mind. Ryan had to work—Japan doesn't professionally observe Christmas—and instead of staying inside feeling sorry for myself, I decided to go on a solo adventure. Any walk alone in Japan felt brave to me, full of unknowns and little wonders.

I followed a steep, winding hill through a quiet neighborhood, half expecting a panoramic view of the city at the top. But what I stumbled upon instead was even more magical: a rose garden in full bloom, tucked between homes, leading up to a small Buddhist shrine.

Two massive stone Buddha heads greeted me. One looked older, the other more recently carved. A bell hung overhead, and a small cabinet held candles and incense. The place radiated care and devotion, and a hush fell over me.

I bowed, letting the sacred stillness settle into my bones. Just as I turned to leave, a woman appeared—clearly arriving to pray. I tried to slip away, but she spoke to me.

"I'm sorry, I don't speak Japanese," I said gently, motioning my intent to give her space.

She kept talking.

I repeated, "Sorry . . . I don't understand," assuming that would be the end of our brief encounter.

But she just spoke more—full sentences, full paragraphs, not like one talks to someone who doesn't speak the language. She wasn't deterred by my confusion. She wasn't asking me to leave. It hit me—maybe she didn't *want* to pray alone. Maybe she wanted to *share* this moment.

So I tried something. I pointed to one of the Buddha heads and asked, "Do you come here every day?"

She beamed. Still speaking in Japanese. Still talking to me like I knew exactly what she meant. Did she know what I said?

At that point, I gave up trying to understand with my mind and chose instead to understand with my heart. I listened. I followed. I mirrored her every move.

She rang the bell, so I rang the bell. We bowed to each Buddha. We lit incense. We stood before each corner of the shrine in reverence. While she spoke, I imagined she was telling me the stories—the meaning, the rituals, the history. And I believed every word I didn't understand.

There was a rhythm to it, a beautiful dance between two strangers. Her sincerity moved me. I was so honored to be invited into her sacred ritual.

That memory reminds me of a story Gabby Bernstein once shared—her first time speaking with a translator. She felt nervous beforehand, unsure how it would go. But when she stepped on stage, she dropped into such a flow led by her intuition that she told the audience to take off their headphones. What followed was her most connected talk yet—because she led with her *presence*.

Her lesson in this was: *"Don't rely on your words, rely on your presence."*

That's what this woman gave me—a presence that transcended language. A soul-level connection that asked nothing of me but openness.

It was the kind of joy that sneaks up on you in the most unexpected places—like a blooming rose garden above the city on a solo walk in Japan.

It's a Christmas I will never forget.

This month, we explore how to deepen connection with the self and others—by letting go of what no longer serves, shifting the quality of your focus, giving generously, and returning to the purity of connection rooted in truth.

This is your chance to experience the magic of authentic connection. There may not be a greater gift in this world than a pure heart-to-heart moment with another living soul.

SPREAD JOY!
Leave a positive review for a local business or service that made your day.

RELEASE TO RECEIVE

Some people come into our lives as blessings. Some come into our lives as lessons.
—MOTHER TERESA

We often hold on to connections out of habit, fear, or memory—even when they quietly drain us. But real joy comes when we make space for what truly supports our hearts. This week, you're invited to let go of relationships or emotional ties that no longer align with who you are becoming. Releasing doesn't mean forgetting—it means choosing to honor your own capacity to receive something more nourishing.

PRACTICE

Find a sustainable seat—on a cushion, chair, or wherever you feel most supported—sitting tall through your spine with eyes softly closed. Connect with your breath and feel every part of you arrive in this space. Once you feel settled, gently bring to mind the relationships in your life. As images of people arise, notice how each feels: which feel nourishing, and which may feel draining, one-sided, or no longer aligned. Simply observe without judgment. When you are ready, return to your breath and bring your awareness back to the present, carrying only the clarity that supports you now.

Write a letter of release to one person (*no need to send it—this is for you!*).

Choose a mantra to support your release. Examples:

- *I bless and release with love.*
- *When I let go, I create space for true connection.*
- *Some people are part of our story, not our destiny.*

REFLECTION

Who are you still holding onto that may no longer belong in your present? What do you need to say or accept to let go? Where can you see how they taught you a key lesson in life so that you may be grateful?

_____

_____

_____

_____

Send them love for all that they taught you as your lives crossed paths. Sit quietly and witness your relationship with them like a movie as you feel gratitude for how that connection is a piece of the puzzle that brought you to where you are now.

_____

_____

_____

_____

Tip: These exercises are not intended for you to ghost people but to prioritize who you choose to engage with regularly. You can still love and care for someone even when you do not interact as much.

Joy Boost

Send a message of gratitude to someone you _are_ still deeply connected with.

WEEK 2

THE CONNECTIONS WE MAKE

What you think, you become. What you feel, you attract.
What you imagine, you create.
—BUDDHA

Our conversations are the threads that weave our relationships. Sometimes, we bond through shared inspiration—and other times, through complaint or worry. This week brings awareness to the energy we bring into connection and the tone we set with our words. Noticing these patterns helps us consciously shift toward relationships that uplift and reflect our values.

PRACTICE
Observe what your closest relationships are rooted in:

- Do you connect through complaints, drama, or negativity? Or through inspiration, joy, growth, or laughter?

Each day, write down one thing you talked about or shared with someone— then reflect on whether it lifted you up or weighed you down.

REFLECTION

What are the recurring themes of your conversations?

_____

_____

_____

_____

What energy do you bring to your connections? What do you want to focus on more?

_____

_____

_____

_____

Mantra

I attract and nurture relationships based on truth, joy, and mutual respect.

THE POWER OF KINDNESS AND SILENCE

Sometimes the most important thing in a whole day is the rest we take between two deep breaths.
—ETTY HILLESUM

Not all connection happens through talking—sometimes, presence speaks loudest. Kindness, like silence, is a powerful and subtle force for deepening relationships. This week, we explore how simple gestures and quiet moments can open the heart and allow in joy, both in our own heart and in others'. How might your presence become a form of love, even when words fall away?

PRACTICE
Practice one simple random act of kindness per day (big or small). This will elevate your mood, energy, and vibration through which you move about the world.

Choose one time each day to be in intentional silence—no phone, no speaking. Just sit or walk quietly, noticing.

In this silence, reflect on: *How am I showing up for others with my presence, not just my words?*

REFLECTION

How does your energy impact others? How does kindness change the way you feel connected or the way others respond to your actions?

_____

_____

_____

_____

How did being in silence feel? Did it help you feel more connected to your inner voice or creativity? Did you notice things about others you otherwise would not have?

_____

_____

_____

_____

Joy Boost

Write a kind, anonymous note and leave it somewhere for someone to find—a car windshield, a neighbor's mailbox, a coworker's office, a public bathroom mirror.

RETURN TO CHILDLIKE OPENNESS

It is a happy talent to know how to play.
—RALPH WALDO EMERSON

Joyful connection is our birthright. Children remind us how natural it is to laugh, play, and simply be with one another without pretense or performance. This week, you're invited to strip away the filters and reconnect with the pure delight of being fully yourself in a relationship. Let this be a week of curiosity, playfulness, and remembering who you were before the world told you to be useful.

PRACTICE

Watch how young children connect—without judgment, expectation, or agenda. Call a friend to talk with no agenda!

Let yourself be silly. Dance. Laugh. Invite play into a conversation or activity.

Set a goal this week to connect with one person without needing to say anything "useful." Just *be* with them.

REFLECTION

How do you feel after allowing yourself to be childlike for a day or week?

_____

_____

_____

_____

When do you feel the most *you* in a connection? How can you create more of that in your daily life?

_____

_____

_____

_____

Mantra

I connect in Truth. My presence is my gift.

BONUS

Picture someone you felt truly connected with this month. Notice what made that connection feel real. Write a sentence that begins, *Authentic connection feels like* . . . and let this feeling guide how you keep showing up in connection with yourself and others.

GRATITUDE PAGES

_____   _____

_____   _____

_____   _____

_____   _____

_____   _____

_____   _____

_____   _____

_____   _____

_____   _____

_____   _____

_____   _____

_____   _____

GRATITUDE PAGES

_____   _____

_____   _____

_____   _____

_____   _____

_____   _____

_____   _____

_____   _____

_____   _____

_____   _____

_____   _____

_____   _____

_____   _____

GRATITUDE PAGES

_____

_____

_____

_____

_____

_____

_____

_____

_____

_____

_____

_____

MONTH 12

LEAD WITH SELF-LOVE

You yourself, as much as anybody in the entire universe,
deserve your love and affection.
—BUDDHA

I opened my eyes and was met with another pair of eyes staring back at me. A woman's face just inches from mine, perpendicular and concerned.

"You just fainted," she told me while she set her phone down, determining she no longer needed to call 911. "Do you know where you are?"

Unfortunately, I did know where I was and that was the worst part. I was mortified.

I was teaching yoga. Emphasis on the *was*.

I, the one who was supposed to be guiding others, had passed out halfway through class. Thirty minutes in and I was on the floor, *out*, in front of a room full of deeply alarmed yogis.

In the seconds that followed, I felt a man wrap a cold towel around my neck. A new student had turned off the heat. Windows were cracked open. The students—my students—had become the caretakers.

I had felt a few warning signs—dizziness and overall weakness—and ignored them. Note to self: Never do that again! I thought I could summon energy for an hour, with the mantra *I can do anything for one hour!* . . . but apparently the heated room was no match for me that day.

As I sat up, I saw all of their eyes on me. I was in new territory. What do I do? What do I say? Through the terror and concern in their eyes, I could tell we were all collectively thinking *Now what?*

Obviously the peaceful mood had been shattered; the irony being that I was subbing because the regular teacher who was seven months pregnant had fainted weeks prior. I didn't have this alibi, and now I'd traumatized this group of students twice!

We all ended with the mutual understanding that class was over but the room was open for personal practice if they so chose. No one did. They all wanted to make sure I was well and could get home safely. One student generously offered to walk me home—she did not have a car but could stay with me the whole way. She didn't know my house was twenty-two minutes away . . . by car.

Their kindness was humbling and yet embarrassment of this moment lingered on my mind and in my body. It clung to me like sweat on a cotton tee. I was disappointed in myself that I hadn't realized I was not fit to teach, that I had missed the signs. And returning to face the same class once I was well gave me shivers.

Later, I told my yoga teacher about the incident and asked how I could better process this moment. She calmly said something I will never forget.

"The issue isn't what occurred. The issue is the shame you're placing on yourself."

Was that a perspective shift!

My view broadened like clouds clearing from the sky as I so clearly saw how the shame I'd been carrying was the problem. She had more . . .

"You're human. Human things will always happen physically as long as we have a body. What if you focused on how you gave those students a chance to lead with love?"

I *so* needed to hear this. Yes, they definitely had led with love and perhaps the yoga practice the universe ordered that morning was leading with love and serving each other.

I needed to drop the self-shaming and lead with love just as my students had shown me. All that was needed in that moment, and every other moment of our life, was the most powerful force that exists: LOVE!

Self-love is the foundation of lasting joy. This final month, and to close the circle on the *Year of You*, we honor ourselves by practicing acceptance from Month 1 and adding on love, authenticity, and compassion.

SPREAD JOY!

Treat yourself intentionally—make yourself a nourishing meal or snack that you truly enjoy, savoring it without distractions. If you have extra, drop off treats to a fire station, hospital staff room, or teacher's lounge.

SPREAD JOY! REFLECTION

How have you felt after spreading joy each month? Did it invoke emotions or a feeling in a specific place in your body? What would it bring to your life to continue spreading joy with random acts of kindness?

_____

_____

_____

_____

RADICAL SELF-ACCEPTANCE

The privilege of a lifetime is to become who you truly are.
—CARL JUNG

We must accept all parts of ourselves—the light and the shadow. In Month 1, you accepted your life situation as it was right then, and this month, you will accept yourself without exception as you are right now. If we cannot love ourselves, then we cannot expect to receive love in return. Being loved is a necessity for all human beings and a core need to feel joy. It starts by sending love to yourself!

REFLECTION
What parts of yourself do you find hardest to accept?

_____

_____

_____

_____

Where do you most judge yourself? How do these parts of you that you judge benefit you?

_____

_____

_____

_____

Where are you resisting love for yourself by judging or rejecting parts of you?

_____

_____

_____

_____

PRACTICE

Write a letter to yourself as a child from the perspective of unconditional love—no fixing, no changing, only accepting. Tell "little you" how great they are with all their strengths and flaws! Give yourself the affirmation (you need or needed then) that you deserve love simply for being alive!

OPTIONAL PRACTICE

Daily mirror affirmations: Look into your eyes and say 10 times to yourself, "I accept you completely. I love you."

Mirror practices can bring up emotion or resistance if a feeling of being unworthy of love runs deep within us. You have worked all year to be able to stand with these feelings—allow them, stand tall, and know that you are worthy of hearing these words.

AUTHENTIC LIVING

To be yourself in a world that is constantly trying to make you something else is the greatest accomplishment.
—RALPH WALDO EMERSON

Remove the masks! Live as your true self, not the version others want you to be. Sorrow at times is our body being tired of the mask (or persona) that we have created for this lifetime. Is it making you tired? Then this is your permission to drop that mask and reveal your true big S Self that is waiting underneath to be seen. Giving yourself permission to be you is the greatest joy that awaits.

REFLECTION
When do you feel most authentic and free?

_____

_____

_____

_____

Who in your inner circle allows you to be fully yourself?

_____

_____

_____

_____

What is one small step you can take this week to express your Truth more often?

_____

_____

_____

_____

PRACTICE

Choose one setting this week to intentionally drop the mask and show up as your most real self (this could be subtle—like speaking your true preference on a decision).

Make a list of qualities you love about your authentic self.

_____

_____

_____

TURNING OBSTACLES INTO SELF-LOVE

The wound is the place where the Light enters you.
—RUMI

We can only ever respond from two places: love or fear. Obstacles test us, inviting us to lean into love rather than retreat into fear. When you reframe hardships as opportunities to love yourself more fully, everything begins to shift.

Yes, this takes courage. It asks you to trust and to step beyond the edge of your comfort zone. But in that space, where love leads the way, you'll begin to notice support, solutions, and strength you couldn't see before. And from that expansion, gratitude blooms into joy when you see the obstacles are for you.

REFLECTION
What past obstacle taught you the most about your own strength and worth?

_____

_____

_____

_____

Consider a current challenge—how might it be guiding you toward deeper self-compassion?

_____

_____

_____

_____

Imagine if every obstacle were here as a teacher—what growth could this one be offering you?

_____

_____

_____

_____

PRACTICE

Write about a difficult experience through the lens of gratitude: Thank you [obstacle], for you helped me learn _____ about loving myself.

You can repeat this sentence for as many lessons as it taught you.

Create a Self-Love Timeline—map key life events and how they contributed to your growth in self-love.

WEEK 4

HEALING AND FORGIVENESS

Forgive yourself for not knowing what you didn't know before you learned it.
—MAYA ANGELOU

Forgiveness is the ultimate act of choosing love—for yourself and for others. It can feel hard to know where to start with forgiveness, and I have found prayer is the most effective way. Prayer is not begging but a message of gratitude for what is and what will be. Offer your stuckness and pain to something greater than you with gratitude, knowing you do not have to do this alone. Forgiveness clears the space where joy has been waiting all along.

REFLECTION

What is your relationship with the word forgiveness? Is it freedom, unachievable, self-compassion, resistance, a process, or even an obligation? How do you want to befriend forgiveness?

_____

_____

_____

_____

Where in your life do you need to offer yourself forgiveness?

_____

_____

_____

_____

What are you ready to release in order to move forward in love?

_____

_____

_____

_____

PRACTICE

Practice the Ho'oponopono prayer to heal old wounds and deepen your relationship with yourself.

Say this silently to yourself daily and every time you feel a twinge of self-judgement, shame, blame, or defeat with full compassion:

- *I'm sorry.*
- *Please forgive me.*
- *Thank you.*
- *I love you.*

Write a forgiveness letter to yourself.

- Allow yourself to be completely honest—don't hold anything back. After a year of reflection, bring to mind the actions, choices, or patterns that felt heavy, dark, or filled with regret. Instead of pushing them away, give them space on the page. Then, offer yourself the profound gift of forgiveness—acknowledging your humanity, your growth, and your readiness to move forward with more lightness and love.

- Notice the lightness that comes when forgiveness softens your heart. Let joy have a place to enter.

- After writing, you may choose to keep it somewhere sacred, read it out loud to yourself, or release it—tear it, bury it, or burn it—as a symbol of letting go.

BONUS

As you close this year's journey, pause to notice who you have become. Breathe into your heart, acknowledging all that has unfolded. Write a single line beginning with *This year of awakening my inner joy taught me . . .* and let it be your gift of wisdom to yourself.

You are love. You are loved.
You are love. You are loved.
You are love. You are loved.

GRATITUDE PAGES

_____   _____

_____   _____

_____   _____

_____   _____

_____   _____

_____   _____

_____   _____

_____   _____

_____   _____

_____   _____

_____   _____

_____   _____

GRATITUDE PAGES

_____   _____

_____   _____

_____   _____

_____   _____

_____   _____

_____   _____

_____   _____

_____   _____

_____   _____

_____   _____

_____   _____

_____   _____

_____   _____

GRATITUDE PAGES

_____
_____
_____
_____
_____
_____
_____
_____
_____
_____
_____
_____

CLOSING

To you, the seeker,

I am so proud of you for completing The Year of You.

It takes courage, devotion, and deep self-respect to walk this path—to show up again and again, and say yes to your own becoming.

Take a moment to look back at where you began.

Feel into how much you've expanded, softened, and stood taller in your truth.

You've done something remarkable: You've built a relationship with yourself that will continue to nourish every part of your life.

Now, I invite you to cycle back to Month 1—not as the person who began this journey, but as someone who has shifted into a higher frequency of awareness, joy, and self-trust. From this new place, you may find new insights waiting, new desires awakening, and new invitations from your heart to rise even further.

This is the rhythm of self-discovery. One mountain leads to another. One layer of joy reveals deeper ones still.

As you continue forward, here is one last practice:

Carry this final question into your days. Let it whisper through your breath, anchor you in the now, and call you into your highest self. Let it ripple outward, not to be answered—but to be lived:

Why do I so effortlessly tap into the wellspring of joy available in every moment, no matter the external noise?

Many of the reflections in this guide come from my own lived experience—lessons I share more intimately in my memoir *The Year of Sarah*. If you'd like to see how these principles play out in real life—with all its messiness and beauty—I'd love for you to journey through my story.

And one day, I hope you'll share your story.

It matters.

It heals.

And I would be honored to hear it.

With love and light,

xo Sarah

FURTHER CONTACT INFORMATION

The Year of Sarah
From Heartbroken to Happy and the Long Distance In Between
Scan the QR code to start reading now!

Stay in touch for more meditations, tips on joy, and book updates:
www.somayogahealing.com/books
Instagram: @somayogaalx & @sarahdeblock_heals

www.ingramcontent.com/pod-product-compliance
Lightning Source LLC
Chambersburg PA
CBHW081656120626
46550CB00010B/2927